D1083399

LUKÁCS'S LAST AUTOCRITICISM

LUKÁCS'S LAST AUTOCRITICISM:

The *Ontology*

by
Ernest Joós

HUMANITIES PRESS
ATLANTIC HIGHLANDS, N.J.

First published in 1983 in the United States of America by Humanities Press Inc., Atlantic Highlands, NJ 07716

©Copyright 1983 by Humanities Press Inc.

Library of Congress Cataloging in Publication Data

Joós, Ernest.
    Lukács's last autocriticism, the Ontology.

    Includes a translation of Die ontologischen Grundlagen des menschlichen Denkens und Handelns, a lecture delivered in Vienna in 1969.
    Includes bibliographical references.
    1. Lukács, György, 1885-1971.   Zur Ontologie des gesellschaftlichen Seins. 2. Ontology. I. Lukács, György, 1885-1971. Ontologischen Grundlagen des menschlichen Denkens und Handelns. English. 1982.
II. Title.
B4815.L83Z8734   111'.092'4   82-1035
ISBN 0-391-02589-9   AACR2

MANUFACTURED IN THE UNITED STATES OF AMERICA

For My Wife

Acknowledgments

The research leading to the composition of this work has been funded by the Social Sciences and Humanities Research Council of Canada and Concordia University. I wish to thank them for their support. I equally thank my graduate assistant, Mr. Stephen Robinson, who carefully read and corrected the manuscript.

Ernest Joós

Table of Contents

Preface

What is the dividing line between a "current event" and history? The probable answer is: time. But how much time? Does a "current event" become history when it moves from one quarter of time, vaguely "contemporary," to one further in the past? It is true that curious and often arrogant newspapermen on the outlook for sensationalism can keep someone alive even after his physical death and prevent impartial history from extending its rightful dominion over him. This matter is of importance to us because it is synonymous with the question in which is raised our main concern: has Lukács been dead long enough for an impartial assessment of his work to be undertaken? Has time come to pass an objective judgment on the man and his work?

Lukács died a decade ago. There can be no interviews to generate animosity between his supporters and opponents or to inflame the curiosity of the dilettante. He remains with us only in his writings and is only wholly with us in the culminating work of his life: the *Ontology*. Is it then possible with the passage of time to read him dispassionately as we do those who, in their lifetimes, evoked a passionate response in all those who read their works?

Of course, there will always be some who cannot take up the work of Hegel, Marx, Freud, or Nietzsche without that sort of emotion which immediately betrays their philosophical faith. But we may still count on a group whose philosophical faith does not blur their vision and who approach even their favorite authors with an attitude similar to that taken up by those who honestly try to understand their faith.

I dare to speak of philosophical faith even in the case of Lukács, who liked to call himself a "Marxist scientist." Such a way of talking is especially justified if we bear in mind his last venture, the *Ontology*. It is not exaggeration to call this work his *philosophical testament*. And, considering it from the point of view of its intent, we may also call it *"Faith seeking understanding."* Those who are shocked by this analogy should turn to the *Ontology* for further explanation. If they have the patience to fight their way through the labyrinth of its pages they will meet with the ghost of Marx in numerous roles — economist, anthropologist, sociologist, philosopher — and in the role that unites all the others, the role of founder of an ontology.

ix

When Lukács sets as his aim "the continuation of Marx", effectively he seeks the understanding of some of the Marxian intuitions that led to what we call nowadays "Marxism." We read on the very first page of Lukács's *Ontology* the statement of his conviction, his philosophical faith, which he means to justify (i.e., render intelligible for others), in what follows: "Niemand hat sich so umfassend wie Marx mit der Ontologie des gesellschaftlichen Seins beschäftigt." ("Nobody has so far occupied himself with the ontology of social being so thoroughly as Marx.") Then he adds: the correctness of this statement, which sounds apodictic, can be verified in the analyses that follow. It is also possible to interpret these words as meaning that Lukács wrote the *Ontology* first for himself, to probe his own soul, to convince himself above all that he was on the right track when he committed himself to Marx.

When we seek to understand our faith, we do not spare it from ciriticism and, indeed, revision, if it does not pass the test. We are therefore justified in calling the *Ontology Lukács's last autocriticism.* Since the *Ontology* contains no reference to contemporary political issues, it is a philosophical confession. Therefore, holding firm to our determination to view Lukács in his *Ontology* only, that is, outside of any political factions, we may achieve a kind of objectivity that could further the understanding of Lukács on the ground of his own merits and not on the ground of his opposition to, or support of, a current political issue in the Marxist camp.

If some might contest, in spite of our intention, the objectivity of our approach, their distrust can find support only in our philosophical method, not in our political affiliation. On the other hand, we have to run the risk of drawing all possible implications from Lukács's ontological positions if we do not want to transgress the rules of ontology. Ontology, as a science of being, dictates its own method and criterion: the search for internal consistency by means of principles (or presuppositions). Our praise and criticism of Lukács find their origin in the ontological method and not in any like or dislike, approval or disapproval of his "philosophy." In other words, we summon Lukács before the tribunal of his own invention: *Marxist ontology.*

Montreal, June 1981.

Ernest Joós

Chapter 1   WHAT IS THE QUESTION?

Is it possible to say anything new about Georg Lukács and his Marxism or is the topic considered closed — and for good reason? The turbulent life of Lukács ended in February 1971, just long enough ago for him to be forgotten as an opponent. However, a controversial figure like Lukács can always be resurrected in one of his historical roles — as a revisionist by those who wish reforms, or as an orthodox Marxist by those who seek in his writings a faithful adherence to the Marxist–Leninist doctrine. The latter may lean heavily on his autocritique, the former on his innovations. Still another Lukács is revived by those who have never been sympathizers, but who, peering at him from the opposite camp, have followed with suspicion and distrust both his political and literary activity.

But do we not see in all these attempts the rehearsal of what has already been said about the man and the politician? Does this repetition provide the assurance, as in *Alice in Wonderland,* that whatever we say three times is true?

Let us therefore assume that everything has been said and that all the facts are known, or, at least, all that are important for us, who look for an encounter with Lukács in the public arena and have no intention of peering into his heart to read the secrets of his sentimental life. If Lukács was a public figure, and it was certainly his intent to be such, then from the flattering remarks of his admirers and the critique of his enemies, we should be able to reconstrue a Lukács in his entirety: meaning a Lukács for all of us and not merely the revisionist, the Marxist, or something else.

Nevertheless, even if the parts are known as in a jigsaw puzzle, it still remains a problem which pattern to follow when we attempt to assemble them. Are we not aware that every portrait is not only an overall picture of the life we wish to reconstrue, but also an overall evaluation of the man whom we are about to portray? Indeed, there is no biography that is free of appraisal even if the author intended to be objective, since the appraisal can well be done by the reader who introduces valuation into his reading through the bias of his interest in the man portrayed. Should we then conclude that it is impossible to be objective because the very "meaning" of

1

events already implies valuation? But should we not admit also that it is equally impossible to place our contemporaries as men of the past on a scale where we could easily read their objective values?

Hence, merely to speak about Lukács would already shatter any hope of being objective and even informative, since words acquire a connotation of value when they appear in a story. On the other hand, even if one finds such expressions as "good" or "evil" objectionable, they can hardly be avoided when the subject is a man of action. Is it not enough to recall Marx's famous eleventh thesis on Feuerbach, which puts praxis above theory? Does praxis not imply at every stage the idea of right and wrong? After Marx, many of his followers intended to change the world; and who can contest that some of these undertakings have been judged by the Marxists themselves as inauthentic, in other words wrong? Therefore, we are back to the idea of valuation, and what is most curious, a valuation according to an undefined criterion. This explains the various versions of Lukács's life and also that the intellectual or the politician receives praise or blame according to the biographer's reference to the right and the wrong, in terms of authenticity. It is easy to find examples for each category, but George Novack's[1] 1978 essay on Lukács should suffice, and it should convince anyone that there is no point in increasing the number of essays on Lukács if we are unable to transcend the partisan bias. Let his admirers and opponents dispute the value of his acts, both political and intellectual.

Since for Lukács self-criticism is no longer possible, certain facts remain, in spite of all, indisputable. We know that he was, as a young man, interested in literature and aesthetics, and later in politics and in Marxism. Shortly before his death in 1970,[2] Lukács recalled his rather late adherence to Marxism, at the age of thirty-five. It is also known that after the short-lived communist regime in 1919 Lukács had to flee Hungary, and that the Hungarian government sought his extradition from Austria for the alleged murder of someone during the reign of Béla Kun. We also know that he was saved by the intervention of European intellectuals, among them Thomas Mann. He became both famous and infamous in 1923, upon the publication of his book *History and Class Consciousness*. Some of his contemporaries, both in the Marxist and non-Marxist camp, consider this book as a watershed in his literary production. Among them we find Lucien Goldmann, who later dedicated a series of seminars to Lukács and compared him to the Heidegger of *Sein und Zeit,* without mentioning more beyond that period as belonging to "his" Lukács. Therefore, Goldmann took no notice of Lukács's self-criticism forty years after the publication of *History and Class Consciousness*. Likewise, Goldmann ignored the fact that the denial of some of the theses contained in

Lukács's famous book coincides with the composition of an extraordinary work for a Marxist—the *Ontology.*

Let us mention another curious event that is known only to a few: during the First World War, in 1917, Lukács applied for a position at the University of Heidelberg, submitting his writings on aesthetics as a *Habilitatio.* [3] This request was accompanied by letters of recommendation, among them one written by a cabinet minister of the Hapsburg regime and an aristocrat. Does it suggest only that the "bourgeois" Lukács had not yet achieved class consciousness, or has it another significance? The University of Heidelberg, after long discussion, rejected his application. But thinking of the possibility that he might have been accepted, does it not make sense to raise the question what would have happened then to Lukács's mission which is clearly visible in all his acts from 1917, the year he wrote his essay *Tactics and Ethics* and took the decisive step of entering the party?

Then, Lukács wrote an unorthodox work for a Marxist—the *Ontology.* Is it not puzzling that in spite of its novelty it received so little publicity? It is true that it has been mentioned, but mostly in newspaper interviews. It was also praised, but only "globally." A work of almost two thousand pages cannot be considered publicized if its content is not articulated in critical essays. It is possible to suggest a reason for this lack of publicity, though it may not be the right one: the *Ontology of Social Being* has not yet been published in its entirety in the original German. Although there are Hungarian, Spanish, and Rumanian translations (and the English translation is supposed to follow soon), these translations cannot reverse the trend, since they are accessible only to few.

But one could also wonder why to attribute importance to this work: especially with reference to Lukács as a man and a Marxist. The fact itself that Lukács worked on his *Ontology* during the last years of his life (from about 1964 to 1971) is an indication of its peculiar place among his works; these are the years when men of Lukács's status and experience write their memoirs or autobiographies. Indeed, a long life of active politics and intellectual commitments spent in the greatest upheavals of history—the First and Second World Wars and the Communist Revolution—would have assured Lukács's memories a place as a best-seller. He could have probably satisfied a mass of readers eager for sensational revelations concerning the inside story of the Kremlin during the Stalinist era, the internal struggles in the Communist Party, the 1956 Hungarian Revolution, and anecdotes about well-known public figures in both the Marxist and non-Marxist camps. Knowing the fluctuations of Lukács's fortune during his long life, the successive attacks and condemnations of his position on Marxism, he would easily have acquired the title of a hero, or a victim of Marxism, in the Marxists' hands. It is not difficult to imagine that he could have received the Nobel Prize for the role he played in widening the scope of Marxism and Marxist humanism. The West needed heroes of that sort, especially during the years of the Cold War—in order to forget them soon after the celebration is over—see the examples of Pasternack and Solzenitzen. Is it not to Lukács's credit to have resisted the temptation of such publicity, which would have served no other purpose than fueling the media for a short time?

Instead, Lukács wrote his *Ontology,* a long and complicated work that even intellectuals will purchase only to *have,* in order to decorate their bookshelves, or from fear of not being considered up-to-date.

The birth of his *Ontology* is in itself an enigma. It represents, in a way, a suspension of time and almost seems to be born out of the transcendence of the dialectic of history. One cannot explain its emergence by historical contexts or the opportunity of the moment, as is the case with *Tactics and Ethics,*[4] where Lukács tries to place the terrorist's act in the flow of events and to explain it by the exigencies of history, or the essays in his *History of Class Consciousness* that have specific reference to specific historical issues.

In retrospect, an impartial observer, who is not a critic of Lukács's Marxism or his revisionism, perhaps not even of his *Ontology* as such, might have the impression that the *Ontology* is a kind of autobiography, more exactly, an *intellectual* autobiography, by which I mean, a reconstruction of Lukács's intellectual history, since there are several ways in which one might write about oneself.

I am tempted, then, to call Lukács's *Ontology* his *intellectual memoirs*—his theoretical autobiography—therefore, his last and authentic autocritique. His *Ontology* is completely in agreement, according to its intent, with Lukács's whole life. Indeed, I would go as far as to say that it sums up Lukács's life work.[5]

Now I venture to say that even if it is impossible to place our contemporaries or men of the past on a scale from which we can easily read their absolute values, we may, in the course of their history, *compare them to themselves,* to their own acts, or rather to their own *intentions.* In this case, the measure will be the *internal consistency of a life.* This way of proceeding is especially commendable when evaluating a man of action. I would then propose for the interpretation and the evaluation of Lukács's career this criterion, which is both *relative* and *universal: relative* in the etymological sense, related to the matter we intend to judge, hence, not exterior to it, hence, not a criterion imposed upon a life and for this reason alien to the objectives and principles that governed the unfolding of its successive stages; *universal,* because such a criterion brings under one common denominator the quickly changing patterns of a personal history and its involvement in the history of its time.

Applying, in this sense, the criterion of *internal consistency of a life* as measure for the evaluation of Lukács's accomplishments, we have, hopefully, shielded ourselves from the accusation of being either for Lukács's revisionism, if the term is correctly used by his opponents, or against Lukács's Marxism, on the ground of our disagreement in principle even with a revised form of Marxism. It should then be clear to all those who follow with me the narrow path of a life—a life that more than once barely escaped annihilation—that it is my intention to create an intellectual atmosphere which will foil all attempts to polarize the debate on Lukács around points of view, which lead nowhere in such a delicate debate, including as it does both political and philosophical issues.

In order to establish some appearance of fairness, I must accept being judged according to the same criterion I propose for the evaluation of Lukács, namely according to the *internal consistency* of my interpretation of the Lukács enigma.

If I am unable to hold firm to this standard, which seems to be the only one to offer some assurance of fairness, or if my readers approach this novelty with suspicion, we will all have missed a chance to demonstrate our good will in attempting to understand Lukács. But before coming to this distressing conclusion we should at least try this method, since, who knows, we may just succeed in our undertaking.

In adopting this method, we may contend that instead of the absolute relativity of all valuations our analysis may reveal the agreement of a life with itself in degrees of the absolute indentity of a praxis with its underlying theory.

Our criterion will also be in agreement with the principle of identity in its ontological application in the following way: in order for an entity to be, it has to be identical with itself (i.e., with the idea it embodies). In ordinary terms this would mean that it is not enough to pretend to be or to simulate being a revolutionary. To be a revolutionary means the agreement of a life with the criterion we customarily associate with a revolutionary.

But this interpretation of an objective criterion, that would have as its kernel *the internal consistency of a life,* might raise objections if our epistemological assumption, namely, that to be a revolutionary means to have definite attributes attached to a life, is contested. The source of this possible objection might be disagreement on the relationship of theory and praxis and their respective importance, or disagreement as to their order of existence or emergence.

Therefore, I have to run the risk of all philosophies, namely that of operating from a presupposition that I may not be able to prove sufficiently. My presupposition is that there is no internal consistency without a theory, that is, there is no praxis without an underlying intellectual framework, or without an underlying implicit intention which assumes the status of a principle. Marcel Proust said that great writers write only one book. By this he meant that they have only one preoccupation, which serves to unify all their partial achievements and which renders even their paradoxes understandable. My task, then, in Proust's terms, is to show that Lukács wrote only one book and to discover that book.

Furthermore, since human beings always construe their social and cultural worlds in some way or other, or, to use a term Lukács employs in his *Ontology,* since man is a "responding" being, we must suppose that those responses originate *somewhere,* and that, being "responses," they are relative to an absolute, which we can call, for the sake of convenience, a principle or principles. In terms of the above, then, it is possible to speak of different levels of consistency: (1) the consistency of acts relative to an intention (or a principle), and (2) the consistency of acts relative to a set of principles. In ideologies, which have the pretence of embracing the totality of human phenomena, the latter should prevail. Therefore, the level of consistency is manifold, and we may speak of both the consistency of acts with a set of principles, and the internal consistency of principles constituting the *Weltanschauung.*

In the case of Lukács, who liked to call himself a Marxist scientist, the criterion of internal consistency becomes the measure of the degree of consistency of both levels—the individual life of the philosopher or the Marxist scientist Lukács, and the degree of consistency of Marxism as a *Weltanschauung* or as a scientific ideology. The two are, in the passionate life of Lukács, intimately interwoven, and, for this reason, his life and his philosophy could be the test of a way of life, such as Marxism. But again, we should stress that this would be the test of the *way of life of a Marxist intellectual,* since to a religious or a political fanatic only the first level of consistency could apply. It is only too common that even people who live by principles lack either the ability or the willingness to test the consistency of their own system of beliefs, i.e., their *Weltanschauung.*

Now, if someone objects that Lukács's Marxism is only one of many possibilities in the line of Marxist ways of life, this objection implies the question of *authentic Marxism.* For outsiders, this issue has much less importance than for those who claim to live by the doctrine that we are accustomed to call, due to its most general characteristics, and after the name of its founder, Marxism. Everybody is aware of the weakness of Christianity or any other religion that originates in the lack of general agreement concerning the basic tenets or the way of life advocated by their founders or promoters.

The Question of Authenticity

At this point, a delicate question has to be raised, namely, that of the *criterion of authenticity*. Not long ago, George Novack published his *Polemics in Marxist Philosophy*,[6] which contains essays on contentious issues and controversial figures in the Marxist camp. This book is only one of its kind, but for the sake of illustrating the disagreement on vital points of Marxism among "authentic" Marxists, it serves our purpose. The essay devoted to Lukács and written as a sort of *In Memoriam* and with the definite intention of judging Lukács once more, or once for all, singles out only one work among the many by the Hungarian Marxist philosopher, and this is *History and Class Consciousness*. As a tribute to the defunct, the work is well chosen, since it is Lukács's best-known writing, although it appeared only in June 1971 in English translation, that is, shortly after Lukács's death. (The French translation dates from 1960, hence does not contain the famous preface of the 1967 edition).[7]

Although Novack's choice—*History and Class Consciousness*—betrays his intent to reopen the trial of Lukács, and under this guise, that of Marxism, it also indicates the interest of posterity both in this work and in the intellectual history of Lukács. Does this work not show, as Novack puts it, the three phases of Lukács as *Marxist theoretician?* Then, the essay can turn out as a debate on authentic Marxism. Therefore, Novack is justified in saying that "this work has had a curious history" (p. 117). We may add that Lukács did too.

It is not my purpose to decide the question of authenticity, since, as can be seen from Novack's book, the Marxists themselves cannot agree among themselves on the indispensable characteristics of a Marxist. My interest in Novack's interpretation is fostered by a difficulty that is even more embarrassing for Marxism to answer than the question of Lukács's authenticity, and that is the relationship of *theory* and *praxis*. We all recall Marx's eleventh thesis on Feuerbach: "Philosophers have interpreted the world in many ways, but what matters is to change it." We read in this solemn proclamation the superiority of praxis over theory, hence one of the essential characteristics of Marxism. Roger Garaudy in his book *Marxism in the Twentieth Century*[8] reiterates the importance for Marxism of "a transition from speculative, utopian ideology to a 'socialist ideology' which has become scientific theory through criticism of 'ideological illusions'" (p. 51). What is the source of this criticism? The answer is obvious: invert the process, that is, "get rid of the illusion of the transcendence of revelation or reason" (ibid), or, in other terms, invert the order in the way suggested by Marx—*praxis* before *theory*—and then try to cope with the difficult task of defining praxis in such a way that theory would be a part of it. The justification of this change from "ideological illusions," synonymous with speculative, utopian ideology, — in a word, with theory, — which corresponds to the interpretation of the world, forced Marxists after Marx to attempt to secure the *internal consistency* of Marxism as *praxis*. And, here we find a distinguished role for Lukács the theoretician.

However, do we not find ourselves in a vicious circle when we stress the priority of praxis over theory and when we wish to present Marxism, as Garaudy does, as a "theoretical expression of this coincidence of a concrete project and a real need, a scientific socialism and the working-class movement" (p. 101)? What follows can hardly take us out of the circular argument: "It (Marxism or the Marxist movement) no longer has a moral character; it is no longer an ideal divorced from life; but is instead fundamentally the development of a praxis" (p. 101).

I have proposed, as the criterion to evaluate Lukács's activity, the internal consistency of his life, and I have run into the problem of authenticity competing with this "measurement."

Then I have tried, with the help of Marxist thinkers, to put my finger on the essential characteristics of Marxism in order to have at least a point of reference with regard to authenticity and I found myself in a circular argument which runs from *praxis* to *praxis* and is supposed to pass through theory. Now, a circular argument can hardly be considered a "scientific idealism", on the other hand, *a praxis that repudiates the moral character of the action has the difficulty of establishing its own authenticity.* There is, indeed, no internal consistency which could be the mark of authenticity without a theory, i.e., without the intellectual framework of praxis. Marx could write, in the *Holy Family* as quoted by Garaudy, that "communists preach no ethical system" and still be consistent with his own thesis, namely, to change the world, since he wanted to change it *at any cost,* and *without any theory.* But those who by some magic want to induce practice to yield a theory are ultimately wrong: they put the cart before the horse. Does this method not lead to the justification of practice, indeed of *any* practice provided its intention is to change the world? Once more, it is Marx who is consistent in his thinking and for the very same reason I mentioned above: he wanted change *at any cost.* "For us, communism is not a stable state which is to be established, an ideal to which reality will have to adjust itself. We call communism the *real* movement which abolishes the present state of things. The conditions of this movement result from the premises now in existence" (*The German Ideology,* quoted by Garaudy, p. 101). Again, the miserable conditions of the working class, and these are the premises, justify the suspension of ethics, and with ethics, also the suspension of theory. In this sense, *all practices are authentic* as long as they are a real movement that intends to abolish the present state of things, i.e., misery. But when Garaudy turns this specific praxis, bound to specific circumstances, into a theory advocating that "the transcending of contradictions no longer, henceforth, comes from outside: communism is no longer a Utopia as a moral system, but the expression of a real movement" (p. 101), he commits the fallacy of deriving a theoretical conclusion from a particular situation. It is doubtful that Marx would have agreed to the abolition of morals as such; therefore it is also doubtful that he would have argued as Garaudy does.

When interpreting Marx in my own way, I do not intend to increase the number of "authentic" interpreters, I only wish to point to a general fallacy perpetrated by Garaudy, and probably by others, which arises out of the unsettled relationship of *theory* and *praxis*. I may affirm with an unusual feeling of certainty that nobody, not even the most authentic Marxist, would be able to deduce from Marx's specific statement advocating the suspension of ethics in a given time and situation, that Marx would have advocated the same form of action or the suspension of ethics, for example, one hundred years later, and in a totally different context.

What I intend to show is that the overemphasis of praxis at the expense of theory could very well turn out to be a non-Marxian premise. The application of the elementary rules of hermeneutics could clear the way to a better understanding of Marx by asking the question about *Marx's intent*. Under this heading it would be possible to establish the internal consistency of his praxis in the same way as I have proposed to interpret his suspension of ethics. But it would be a different problem if we tried to establish the internal consistency of the Marxian theory as it has been elaborated by his disciples. I dare to venture an answer that may not be acceptable to most of my Marxist colleagues: that Marx never intended to construe a consistent philosophical doctrine which would also include a *theory of praxis*. What we call the Marxist theory, or the Marxist philosophy, is a later product, an ambition that surpassed the intention of Marx, who, pressed by circumstances prevailing in the beginning of the nineteenth century, wanted to change the world. However, since "Marxism" is now a reality due to the number of thinkers who attribute to themselves that name, it is perfectly justifiable to speak of the *internal consistency* of their Marxism and in this context of Marxist philosophical theories, including the *theory of praxis*. It is therefore, not without reason that the *theory of praxis* acquires a great importance—the innumerable comments on this topic are a sufficient proof of this.

Marxist authors display in this exercise a considerable skill: a good example of this is Althusser's *theory of praxis,*[9] since it shows both the ingenuity needed to tackle the issue and the necessity for such a theory.

I am tempted to say that this endeavor is, indeed, the indication of a need for a theory *per se*. The question is only how to find it in a way different from all other existing theories.

Readers accustomed to thinking according to principles can judge for themselves the accomplishment of Althusser. I only point to a key notion in Althusser's interpretation of the *theory of praxis;* this notion by itself expresses all the difficulties the "faithful" Marx interpreters encounter when they wish to *extend* Marx beyond himself. This notion is the *theoretical practice.* Its elaboration is found in Althusser's book *For Marx,* in the chapter entitled, *"On the Materialistic Dialectic."*

"By theory . . . I shall mean a specific form of practice," he writes, "itself belonging to the complex unity of the 'social practice' of a determinate human society. Theoretical practice falls into the general definition of practice." It works on a raw material (representation, concepts, facts) which is given by other practices, whether "empirical," "technical," or "ideological." "In its most general form theoretical practice does not only include scientific theoretical practice, that is, 'ideological' theoretical practice (the form of 'knowledge' that make up the prehistory of a science, and their 'philosophies' " (p. 167). But, surprisingly, Althusser complains that "ideology is not always taken seriously as an existing practice . . . The existence of a *theoretical practice* is taken seriously even more rarely . . ." (p. 167). One wonders, then, *who takes practice as theory seriously?* And what is even more disturbing, how do we designate the one who has the right to speak of authenticity? If Althusser and his followers are the only ones, do they not look themselves like sectarians in the bosom of an old religion? And what to say if Althusser himself becomes a renegate of his own religion? Does he not write some years later that the definition of philosophy as *theoretical praxis* is unilateral, hence incorrect?[9A]

It is needless to refer to other attempts to clarify the issue of the theoretical practice or the theory of practice, since an authoritative source, the *Philosophisches Wörterbuch,*[10] confirms the importance of a theory of praxis without being able to be more explicit than Althusser. However, one thing strikes the reader: specific references to Marx are extremely scarce, and, with regard to Marx's definition of praxis, almost nonexistent, in this otherwise highly scientific and reliable work.

This lack of unanimity and even lack of clarity in the definition of praxis will have a far-reaching consequence on the discussion of authenticity relative to the interpretation of Marxism in general and to social, political, and revolutionary praxis in particular.

On this ground, I continue to argue that the discussion about the authenticity of Lukács or other Marxist thinkers remains a paradox as long as the theoretical basis of authenticity is not clearly established.

And this cannot be done as long as Marxist thinkers endeavor to deduce theory from practice, i.e., persist in generalizing the particular, and in trying to raise the concrete, *without the intermediary of a theory*, to the level of the universal.

Now, we read in Novack that "ordinary professors of philosophy appeared like petty provincials beside . . . [Lukács]." This "millionnaire of learning" moved with consummate ease through the corridors of Western philosophy and dealt with contemporary problems of thought in a powerful analytic *manner* (p. 119). Is it any wonder, then, that Lukács noticed the theoretical weaknesses of Marxism and that he made the correction of these shortcomings the purpose of his life? But his critics have forgotten to credit him for not blaming Marx for these shortcomings.

It is obvious that my difficulty with Novack's interpretation of *History and Class Consciousness* arises from the notion of praxis as applied to Lukács and more specifically from the unspecified theoretical grounds that serve as basis for his criticism of Lukács. Indeed, Novack becomes the victim of his own criterion of authenticity, which suffers from the same logical shortcomings as the one I mentioned, namely, the elevation of the particular, without mediation of a theory, to the rank of universal. Does he not refer to Engels and Lenin as the criteria of a theory? If the interpretation of particular men cannot be questioned by reason, are not reduced to sitting at the feet of oracles and prophets? What happens, in this case, to the claim of Marxism to being a scientific ideology?

"Theorizing" of such kind does not go unpunished, and we can now quote Novack against himself. While arguing the "idealistic deviations of Lukács," does Novack not recognize Lukács's orthodoxy with reference to the emphasis on the theory of alienation even before Marx's early philosophical papers had been made available? Could we not say, without being suspected of writing an apology for Lukács, that it was his *theoretical* understanding of Marx which made him capable of projecting alienation, ahead of his time, onto the canvas of history? Of course, "the idealistic deviations of Lukács in the most general field of Marxist theory went hand in hand with the unrealistic strategy he then advocated for the proletarian vanguard" (p. 120).

Should we not remind Novack of the two levels of his arguments? Had he realized the distinction between the particular and the universal, he would have granted Lukács an *Aufhebung,* namely, his intent to serve the cause of the proletariat. Lukács's flight into "pure thought" on the "level of rarified abstraction"—which was, we assume, a residue of his "grounding in classical

German philosophy," as Novack calls it—enabled him to track down Marx's *Ungedachte* in *Kapital* and to make it explicit in the form of the concepts of alienation and reification "in the revolutionary criticism of the capitalist system," thus demonstrating the force of the theory which is bound to operate on the *level of the universal;* but on the other level, that is, the application of a theory to the particular, namely Lukács's venture into the field of history, made him liable to errors and criticism, and, as could happen to anyone, even to Marx, he made miscalculations concerning the outcome of historical evolutions. Once more, we witness in these examples the fallacy of reasonings on authenticity when they are grounded in an ill-defined *theory of praxis.*

In the appraisal made by Novack, Lukács becomes victim of an inconsistency which characterizes Marxism in general—the inability to coordinate *theory* and *praxis.* Nevertheless, Lukács is not the only victim of this inconsistency. His readers and admirers will not escape the same fate, since they will be liable to Lukács's crimes when trying to capitalize on Lukács's deviations.

Novack is in a good position to be able to refer to Lukács's own complaints "about this abuse of his early, outgrown and erroneous version of Marxist theory. His book is too useful," says Novack, "for those who want to 'trim Marx's beard' " (p. 118).

Under such circumstances would it be possible to avoid this pitfall and evade the suspicion when writing on Lukács of being only one of those "trimming Marx's beard"? Definitely not, if the rules of the game remain as loose as they are in the *theory of praxis.* I would not go so far as to say that under the old law of authenticity anyone can be anyone's accuser; but this is almost the case, so great are the differences between the conception of authenticity in different camps. Therefore, we could only gain by trying to resort to a criterion where the emphasis would be not on whether Lukács is an authentic Marxist, but whether there is, in spite of the contradictory judgments, *an authentic Lukács.* This question is only the rewording of the *internal consistency* of a life which I proposed earlier as criterion of evaluation for Lukács's activity, both political and intellectual.

This undertaking presents no small challenge. Although conscious of the difficulty, I wish to present to the reader the authentic Lukács. This approach tones down the ambition of reaching a conclusion in the difficult matter of who is authentic himself.

However, to support my venture with plausible arguments, I shall recount an instance from Lukács's life that confirms also the necessity of considering the internal consistency of his life, rather than who is an authentic Marxist, as criterion of judgment. It renders enigmatic the much publicized self-criticism found in the preface of the 1967 edition of *History and Class*

Consciousness, and also Novack's assurance when he states that "the commentary in the preface presents *his real views"* (p. 120, italics mine).

Internal Consistency as Authenticity

Is it not strange that shortly before Lukács's death, a selection of his works—from the earliest politcial writings, such as *Tactics and Ethics,* to the very last one, his *Ontology*—was published in Hungarian under the title, *Utam Marxhoz "My Road to Marx"*[11] and, although essays from *History and Class Consciousness* form the core of the first volume, the rectifications contained in the famous preface of 1967 were not considered by Lukács himself part of his *Way to Marx?* Nevertheless, he mentions them in the preface to this collection. This constitutes the second version of his confessions and it takes a peculiar form.

While suggesting that *History and Class Consciousness* reflected his preoccupation during the revolutionary period of 1917 and the event that followed the Hungarian Communist Revolution and also his *"messianic and sectarian convictions,"* Lukács rejects the criticism levelled against some of the deviations in this book. In order not to slip into a partisan interpretation of his position on the crucial issue, I reproduce Lukács's own view so that the reader may have a chance to compare it to the famous preface of 1967 of *Geschichte und Klassenbewusstsein.*

When so doing I must call attention to a fact that sounds strange to those who know Lukács only from secondary sources; namely, that Lukács should have made a second kind of autocriticism: to quote Kostas Axelos, translator of *Histoire et conscience de classe,* the autocriticism of his style.

On the other hand, should we not say that Lukács's style helped him to retract his errors only to confirm them in a different way, as is the case in the preface to his *My Road to Marx:*

> The weak parts of my undertakings become clear now that we examine them without prejudice. First of all, one has to mention the conception of Marxism as a theory applicable solely to society. Of course, the official critics of that time (Gyeborin, Rudas, etc.) wrongly criticized even the wrong assertions of the book and in such a way they have often directed their attacks to something which was latent in them as an unconscious progressive tendency at that time yet improperly formulated. (What I meant was) that we cannot have a scientific foundation of the dialectic of social evolution unless we unfold *historically, by way of an ontology,* the highest degree (the social being) from the categories of natural being and not vice versa, namely taking these categories of

natural being as models for the elaboration of the laws of higher forms of being" (pp. 21-2).

The first part of this statement stresses the *historical* method, while the last part reaffirms the great importance of the categories of natural being, i.e., ontology.

Lukács wrote the preface to *My Road to Marx* when his *Ontology* was already completed, or at least written down. In its historical part we find a definition of general ontology, but in different, even contradictory, terms. "Social being has several domains and all of them seem to be subject to the same kind of necessity and order of laws as nature itself."[12]

Further, he confirms his principle by saying: "general ontology, or to say the same thing in a concrete way, the ontology of inorganic nature as foundation of every being is general in this sense that there is no being whose ontological foundation does not originate somehow in inorganic nature."[13]

One may argue in favor of Lukács's saying that in the two contexts he did not face the same problem; however, the role of nature understood as the *material* foundation of all categories is clearly maintained in both. Now let us consider the second part of his statement in the preface of *My Road to Marx,* where he seems to maintain that *History and Class Consciousness* was often right, even in its wrong assertions; for example, stressing too much the importance of the historical and social method. This fluctuation of Lukács's thought stems from his uneasiness when confronted with the internal consistency of materialism and that of an ontology. He himself seems to be split between the difficult fidelity to Marx and materialism and the exigencies of ontology. This split will become even more evident later in the elaboration of his theses in the *Ontology.*

For us, considerable difficulty in the interpretation of his statement is created by the meaning of key notions, such as *historical* and *ontological*. We do not claim that a translation could perfectly render the ideas of a philosopher. Therefore, we wish to add that perhaps Lukács let himself be dragged along his long sentence having in mind an ontology that would become a compromise capable of uniting both *historical* and *natural being,*[14] or, to say the same in conventional terms, *becoming* and *permanence.* If this was his intention, we may rightly question how ontology, which has to determine the criterion of a being, hence that of some sort of permanence, can become *historical.*

We dare to venture the opinion that the term *historical,* along with *dialectical,* can often be considered almost as jargon in Marxist philosophical writings; therefore, a sort of concession to Marxist *ideology.* Whenever this is the case, these expressions serve only to increase the volume of grandiloquence, which is a dangerous ingredient in ontology, a science characterized by its ascetic rigor and colorless expressions. It is in this respect that Lukács's *Ontology* differs so much from other ontologies. The lack of rigor in his terminology increases the hazards of interpretation, especially when we are faced with purely philosophical texts, such as the *Ontology*. Of course, this shortcoming should not be blamed on Marx, whom Marxist philosophers continue to quote in support of their speculations. It is questionable whether Marx really had the ambition to construe a philosophical system that would embrace and synthesize the various disciplines, as his followers wished to do. The more critical we are of the incommensurate ambition of "Marxist philosophers," the more we value the modesty of Marx, and raise even the issue whether Marx really wanted to be "continued," "completed," and "brought up-to-date," as Lukács puts it.[15]

The statement "ascetic rigor and colorless expressions" should also be explained. An ontology is measured, as Whitehead says, by its *applicability;* its applicability, on the other hand depends on the logical consistency of its principles. Lack of rigor destroys the consistency of an argument, thus rendering its applicability hazardous. Therefore, in order to render justice to the novelty of the *Ontology* of Lukács, it is not enough to refer to the main tenets of this theoretical work; the essential is to examine their implications, which then reveal their logical consistency and their actual applicability to the categories of being. This is the only way to discover and evaluate Lukács's innovations which are usually buried under his wordiness.

Ontology considers entities according to their most common denominator—*being*: in the secton on ontology I shall further develop this theme. Here, I alluded to this science only to stress the importance of rigor in philosophical writings. After all, Lukács's success in carrying out his task to secure the internal consistency of Marxism will depend on his ability to formulate a theory of praxis. This undertaking requires, then, the art of seeing the implications of terms, including the ones I label simply jargon.

The preface to *My Road to Marx* was not yet a test case for Lukács. His own ambiguities only helped to camouflage his intention to let his "comrades" know that after all, he—and not the so-called orthodox, i.e., *authentic Marxists*—was correct.

Lukács's neglect of the dialectic of nature and his "ambiguous" repentence contribute only to perpetuate the confusion around the all-important ontological problems related to the interpretation of *social being*. Furthermore, we may add, without unduly exploiting this lukewarm repentence, that Lukács quickly finds consolation in his *right* understanding of reflection *("Widerspiegelung")* by introducing into this theory man's teleological, i.e., purposive, reaction, to material circumstances. This leads, according to Lukács, to the proper reflection between nature and society, and, we may add, to another transgression of the laws of orthodox Marxism.[16]

Lukács does not fail to credit himself with a theoretical success, namely, "the progressive possibility" opened up, thanks to this book, in the *correct interpretation* of reflection, although *concrete issues received incorrect solutions.*[17]

But again, Lukács has not foreseen that his solution in bridging the gap between man and nature through correct reflection leads to a most serious ontological problem, namely, to the order of appearances of phenomena or their ontological priority and their ontological foundation; for example, that of consciousness. To sum up, this autocriticism is a strange mixture of pride and repentence that gives Lukács an opportunity to stress his prophetic insight in *History and Class Consciousness.* If we already use such loaded terms as *prophetic insight* we should also note that the kind of prophecy Lukács is praised for originates in the *proper understanding of principles, i.e.,* in *theory.*

But at the same time, Lukács confesses that, after the condemnation of the Blum thesis, he discovers *Marx's Critique of Political Economy.* The reading of this work convinces him that instead of producing a patchwork, he must now reformulate his basic conceptions concerning Marxism. Then, he sets aside *History and Class Consciousness* in order to return to the same problems later, when he has acquired the necessary knowledge to answer them.

Lukács is a *recidivist* in every sense of this term. As promised, he returns to the problems dealt with in the much-debated book, but only to confirm that, in essence, he was right. Unwilling to engage in a political debate, I insist on the fact that in agreement with Lukács's own definition of his life work—to give a theoretical foundation to Marxism—the *essential* for him is that which constitutes the framework of praxis and this is found in his last work, the *Ontology.*

In sum, this kind of "autocriticism" is a strange confession of the errors of the past. It stresses rather the implicit truth and the progressive nature of earlier deviations. But one must admit at least this much; that Lukács remains consistent in his actions. The same characterizes the rest of the text devoted to *History and Class Consciousness.*

While pleading for himself—saying, "*History and Class Consciousness* comes in serious conflict with certain prejudices existing in Marxism"—Lukács adds, as if he wanted to soften his position: "naturally without being able to offer satisfactory philosophical solutions." Among Lukács's failures has been his inability to place labor in the center of his analysis of the capitalist system.[18]

On this ground, we may wonder, then, which Lukács was the authentic Lukács? The one who wrote in 1967 his self-criticism and published it in German, or the one who did not find it important to include this same preface in his *Road to Marx* in Hungarian? Of course, some would find it improper to speculate on his reasons for first writing this preface, then later omitting it. There remains only the alternative of exploring further how the notion of *internal consistency* can help us to determine, with acceptable accuracy, which was the authentic Lukács: the one who confessed his errors or the one who failed to "improve," or still another Lukács, who affirmed shortly before his death that he understood Marx better than anyone? In this case, how to interpret the "three phases" in his "evolution" mentioned by Novack with reference to *authenticity?* And why could the one which contained his idealistic deviations not be *authentic?* Putting the question in such a way, we need not give reasons for Lukács's self-criticism or for other paradoxes in his life that could only foster disagreement in partisan camps and increase the passion that prevents formation of an objective judgment on the man and his work.[19]

Theory and Praxis—How They Introduce an Almost Incurable Bias into the Discussion of Lukács

It is laudable to undertake to overcome the dualism of subject and object or theory and praxis. This is the merit Lucien Goldmann attributes to Lukács in his work, *Lukács and Heidegger.*[20] But should not another merit no less important be added to these pairs of opposites, to give thinkers new fields where they can display their ability—that is, the dualism of man and politician or thinker and politician? If someone objects that it is already included in the second, theory and praxis, we will have some difficulty arguing that this is not entirely the case because theory corresponds correctly to the activity of a thinker and praxis describes adequately that of the politician. Then, we could even argue that the "political thinker" would perhaps be the one to realize the desired unity, since political thinking is done either in view of explaining what has happened or what is expected to happen. However, such an interpretation may follow a different ideological bias: that is to say, a praxis meant to change the world can have various theoretical antecedents which necessarily lead to various forms of praxis and various forms of politcial patterns. Hence any "abstract" theorizing about the unity of theory and praxis fails on the stumbling block of the *"concrete,"* because the *"concrete,"* that is, actual political realization, offers itself to criticism and, what is more disastrous for "pure thought," it does so from different theoretical points of view. This state of affairs leads us to believe that all attempts at reducing theory to practice or vice versa are doomed to fail or that they inevitably become, from the very beginning, ideologies with a built-in bias either for the conservation of existing praxis or the introduction of new ones. As a result, critics of a theory or a praxis place themselves in respectively different positions according to their own ideological bias, and consequently the same act or the same person may be the object of unconditional praise or unconditional blame depending on the issue under discussion. Under such circumstances it is almost impossible to come to any agreement on what constitutes the *objective* content of a theory or a praxis and, as a result, the thinker or the politician receives recognition for reasons alien to his merits or demerits. As usually happens in such cases, praxis takes precedence over theory, because theory is evaluated only according to its possible realization in a social, political, or economic institution. This is how we come to a very common bias, the *partisan view.*

Georg Lukács received much praise and as much criticism, and it seems that both the praise and the criticism were motivated by partisan considerations. Partisan considerations, on the other hand, are usually related to praxis or to an ideology meant to be implemented. Thus, it is easy to understand why the purely theoretical part of every "political" thinking suffers the most, or, in other terms, receives the least recognition. This is exactly the case with Lukács. As an example, I have mentioned Novack and Goldmann, both belonging to the Marxist camp. Novack's explanation of Lukács after his death is totally centered on the latter's controversial book, *History and Class Consciousness.* On the other hand, the praise of one of Lukács's admirers, Goldmann, is limited to Lukács's earlier works up to the middle of the 1920s, hence a long period of feverish intellectual and political activity is left intentionally in the dark, again for practical purposes: Goldmann limits Lukács to what Goldmann wishes to keep, that is, to appropriate from Lukács's teaching; Novack, on the other hand, confines Lukács to what Novack wishes to eliminate from Lukács's "influence."

Such practices, to say the least, contribute little to the understanding of the authentic Lukács. Furthermore, they continue to cultivate the mystery around a man whose intention was certainly not to become a mythical figure. If anything, it is definitely his effort to understand and clarify his own commitments that is to the credit of Georg Lukács.

Let us close these remarks on a positive note for Lukács. Considered in its entirety, Lukács's life points towards an *internal consistency* governed by principles that Lukács has never completely relinquished. Thus, in spite of the digressions in his political and philosophical career, there is a sort of continuity that is made evident in his ontological preoccupation. Of course, his preoccupations are not always explicitly ontological. In order to make this continuity visible, we should perhaps call his preoccupations *theoretical.* We have to praise his remarkable lucidity when he wrote in the preface of his *My Road to Marx* that he was aware of the fact that there could be no way of correcting some of the errors in his *History and Class Consciousness* without the reformulation of its basic conception: "I realized that it would be wise to start anew the whole work and to set aside globally the methodical errors of *History and Class Consciousness* and by so doing to liberate myself and gain the necessary intellectual freedom to return, at a later date, to the correct answering of these very same problems."[21] Indeed, Lukács returned to these very same problems and with a basically new conception which gave rise to his *Ontology*. Therefore, leaving out the greatest part or the ultimate attempt, the *Ontology,* to secure the internal consistency of his thought constitutes not only a disservice to Lukács, but also to posterity, namely, to his readers, or what is even more important, to his disciples. This is the main reason I wish to center the debate on Georg Lukács around his last work, the *Ontology.*

Types of Internal Consistency

When we speak of the internal consistency of a life, we unavoidably speak out of moral considerations, or, at least, from the standpoint of some form of philosophy of action. Henceforth, we run the risk of being moralists, a label that is hard to bear in the age of positivism. But this approach is justified when applied to Lukács, whose main preoccupation towards the end of his life was precisely to work out an ethics for Marxism. What is an ethics if not the reconciliation or *Aufhebung* of theory and praxis? In other words, ethics is the intellectual or conceptual framework of praxis; we can even say that ethics is a theory of praxis and, in this form, the real *Aufhebung* of theory and praxis. At the end of his life, Lukács dared to affirm that praxis itself demands the elaboration of a Marxist ethics.[22]

But again, the core of this theory of praxis has to be a theory, which inevitably inverts the order established by Marx's eleventh thesis on Feuerbach. Hence, from the start, Lukács is, and we with him, in the wrong. In Novack's terms, we are both victims of the same tendency—the tendency to intellectualize: "Lukács approvingly cited his old teacher, the neo-Kantian Heinrich Rickert, who said that materialism was "inverted Platonism." Whereas for him the dialectic was proletarian, he considered the materialist position to be essentially metaphysical and bourgeois" (p. 121).

This quotation contains the two original views of Lukács: his love of theorizing and his conviction that dialectic is limited to the social and historical element (which implies already, without mentioning it, the negation of Engels's famous dialectic of nature). Novack sums up Lukács's sins in the following terms: *"History and Class Consciousness* sets forth the premise that

Marxism is exclusively a theory of society, a philosophy of human history" (p.121).

If we were unable to find any other internal consistency in Lukács's life, we could still say that his successive self-criticisms did not prevent him from remaining recidivist, that is, liable to commit the two original sins of theorizing and limiting dialectics to the social element. These characteristics may exclude him from the ranks of authentic Marxists, but it is difficult to contest that these are exactly the ones that make him *authentic Lukács*. If Lukács sinned against "authentic" Marxism, then he did it consistently and to the very end of his life.

On another level, Lukács's original sin, his conviction that dialectic is limited to the sociohistorical element, explains his commitment to the Marxist praxis and his endeavor to make this praxis *intelligible*. On this point he has never changed his views and he does not refrain from criticizing his fellow Marxists, even before his death, for neglecting and obstructing, out of sheer opportunism, the development of theoretical work in Marxism. One of the obstacles, in the way of promoting this theoretical work — says Lukács is a form of opportunism that he calls "tacticism." This consists in the employment of the intellect for momentary or daily needs, instead of using it for the critique and improvement of practice in general. The other form of opportunism, which, from the point of view of authenticity is even more serious, manifests itself in the neglect of publishing Marx's complete works. Up to this day, 120 years after the publication of the *Communist Manifesto* and 50 years after the foundation of the first Marxist state, many of Marx's writings — among them the notes he made before writing *Capital* — are covered with dust in inaccessible archives.[23]

Theoretical endeavor on the one hand, and a reckless attitude when involved in revolutionary praxis, on the other hand, are characteristic of Lukács. The distinction between revolutionary praxis and praxis in the ordinary sense, what we can call ethics, proves Lukács's realism on the level of political action and his love for theorizing.

The two levels of praxis also fit into the frame of *internal consistency:* the internal consistency of the life of the politician governed by an *intention* to bring about the desired change, and the internal consistency of a doctrine that is designed to insure the permanence of a state of affairs considered ideal for humanity as a whole. Of course, intentions are motives that cannot have logical or scientific justification, because they belong to the category of conception of life, or *Weltanschauung*. The presuppositions of conceptions of life are always irrational. But the doctrine built upon them also requires an internal consistency that can be called "second-level internal consistency," and it differs from intentions. Now, a *Weltanschauung* such as Marxism is under the obligation of justifying its intention; an ordinary religious or cultural *Weltanschauung* does not have to do this. It is the attribute "scientific," then, which creates the most difficulty for Lukács and other Marxist theoreticians, because they have to turn a praxis into a *scientific theory,* or at least they have to rationalize it, and this is not required of a cultural *Weltanschauung*.

Chapter 2   WHICH IS THE AUTHENTIC LUKÁCS?

Any impartial observer would concede that the problem of authenticity is an insoluble question for Marxists (as well as for Christians, not to mention other examples). With the exception of the fanatics, who consider themselves the guardians of the absolute truth, the issue would not be debated and would even be avoided. As Novack's example shows, the more-or-less violent settlement of differences exists only in partisan camps. For others, Marx has become more a symbol of social change that may have different aspects according to different circumstances than the prophet who worded his message in unambiguous terms.

At the end of his life, Lukács declares enthusiastically: "We mark the beginnings of a real Marxist renaissance. More and more people recognize that Marxism provides the only workable solution to the current world crises. If we wish to guarantee its authority in all fields, then we have to endeavor to transform it in such a way that it may be respected by all."[1] This means, indeed, that pluralism in the Marxist camp is tolerated, if not encouraged; this leads to the so-called eurocommunism, and Lukács can be considered as its forerunner. This state of affairs, however, does not dispense any Marxist from trying to secure the internal consistency of the doctrine once a program for social change, i.e., praxis, and for the philosophical justification of this change, i.e., theory, is announced. For an intellectual who commits his life to a doctrine, the presuppositions that constitute the core of the doctrine create binding logical necessities that compel the adherent to establish the *internal consistency of his way of life.* Hence, in this sense, although it is not possible to come to terms with authenticity in Marxism as a universal designation of a form of praxis, it becomes imperative for every Marxist intellectual to secure the authenticity of his own *praxis,* and this he can achieve only through a *theory.*

Having given up the notion of authenticity in absolute terms, we have come to test some notions relative to a praxis construed on a theory which may differ in certain respects from one individual to another. The difference will lie in the choice of presuppositions as essential elements and in the abil-

22

ity to mold a praxis, or a way of life, in such a way that the doctrine shaped around these essential elements would answer the particular questions originating in our social, political, cultural, and ethical preoccupations. It is obvious that those questions vary according to the education or degree of intelligence and inner experience of any individual engaged in this praxis; hence this revised form of authenticity will be applicable to any member of the large Marxist family. However, beside its *applicability,* mention should be made of its *necessity,* namely, that a way of life publicly accepted, as is the case for Lukács and many others committed to an ideology, will be part of the *internal consistency* of their lives, and also part of their *intellectual obligation.* Having reached this point, it is hardly possible to avoid answering the next question, which becomes equally pressing for an intellectual, namely, what others, following their footsteps, could expect from such a way of life. That part of an *intellectual obligation* can be worded as *intellectual honesty.*

Thus a life (in the present case, the life of Lukács) which has been engaged, out of enthusiasm, sympathy, or love, to change the world into whatever form of social praxis, should be reexamined, as a matter of intellectual honesty, in the light of the presuppositions visible in the doctrine with regard to the value that could be created in the new way of life. If few revolutionaries arrive at this stage of theoretical foundation of praxis, cases such as Lukács's are all the more valuable.

His long life gives examples for every instance of this natural evolution dictated by enthusiasm and sympathy to establish in the world a new form of social praxis. Intellectual honesty demands that one provide a theoretical foundation for this praxis and crown it with an ethics flowing from the exigencies of intellectual honesty and designating the values on which the new social order would construe its society.

We are fortunate that Lukács was able to see his life in retrospect and to express in unambiguous terms the objectives he pursued during his whole life, viz., *to give a theoretical foundation to Marxism as praxis.* His aim, translated into the "language" of Marxism, was *to reconcile theory and praxis.*

If at the age of eighty-five Lukács kept repeating that this was his life's project, we have no choice but to believe it and to confront his life with this objective in order to judge its authenticity. For authenticity is not an abstract notion; the authenticity of a faith is measured by the conformity of the believer's life with this faith.

Lukács himself indicated that this is the appropriate standard. He said: "I committed myself to serve the Dictatorship of the Proletariat and I had to account for my acts to the same (idea)."[2]

But what is more striking than any statement is the conformity of Lukács's life to the purpose of giving a theoretical foundation to Marxist praxis. If we understand his life in these terms, we can account for his aberrations as an intellectual. This will also explain his misjudgments of his contemporaries.

How did Lukács understand the theoretical foundation of Marxist praxis?

No one should be surprised that I stress Lukács's role as *intellectual* in the shaping of a theory of praxis. One may easily be a "man of action," but one becomes a theoretician by seeking, through reflection, justification for the action. It may be objected that all men of action have a reason for acting the way they do. Let us, then, distinguish two types of reasons or grounds; those cited to justify an individual or collective action, but at the same time lacking completely the coherence conferred by a body of principles or a theory, and those related to and flowing from a *theory*.

At a very early stage of his commitment to Marxism, Lukács raised a crucial issue facing all those revolutionaries, who want to change the world without first interpreting it, the issue of *terrorism*.

The essay Lukács wrote at the time he entered the communist party bears the title, *"Tactics and Ethics."*[3] This title, rendered in the language of our problematic, reads as follows: *Praxis and Theory*. Like any body of theory, ethics attempts to elaborate principles that are internally consistent, rules that do not contradict one another. *Ethics is the theory of social praxis* and is in this sense the guardian of equity and justice. *Terrorism is the suspension of ethics,* i.e., the suspension of theory to allow an *irrational* act, an act that is an *exception* to the rule. But in so doing ethics must rationalize even its exceptions, and this implies the provision of a theoretical basis for the irrational: in our case, the terrorist's act. This theorizing must take into account the notion of freedom—ethics' fundamental problem. Hence, in this early writing we can witness Lukács's brave struggle for consistency along the lines of presuppositions that he has borrowed from dialectical materialism. In all our human ventures, especially in those that concern our social and political praxis, freedom stands out as the essential element that conditions even theory—for it is at the heart of rationality—and therefore we will examine the theory of political praxis in the next chapter, subtitled *"Terrorism and the Notion of Freedom."* This approach may bring out the main issues of our problematic, whose starting point is, as we have mentioned already, the *intention* to systematize Marxist praxis, more specifically, a praxis as understood by one of the members of this political group, since the notion of authentic Marxist praxis had to be abandoned. Although this theorizing is carried out by an individual member of the Marxist group, it will have repercussions on the Marxist doctrine in general, because the failure of an individual adherent to bring about the desired internal consistency indicates that a threat looms over the entire venture and may point towards the weaknesses of Marxism itself.

This is one of the reasons why Lukács's life and activity become so important to the intellectual commmunity. Lukács is a test case exactly *because he theorizes*. Having abandoned the dangerous course of judging Lukács according to a universal standard of Marxist authenticity, I am at ease in arguing out with him the issues that are the common preoccupation of any intellectual interested in the shaping of our world, or its interpretation.

In this context, there cannot be any ill-feeling on the part of either Marxist or non-Marxist inquirer into the problems of human affairs. Rationality as common denominator sets the criterion of truth regarding the discussion of these matters, and intellectual honesty governs the ethics of the dialogue.

It is in this atmosphere of mutual interest and mutual respect that the dialogue with Lukács becomes not only possible, but also fruitful.

The first leg of this intellectual journey into the realm of personal commitment will be, then, *Tactics and Ethics*.

Before entering into the systematic analysis of *Tactics and Ethics,* let me justify my choice and also the emphasis of this little treatise. When Lukács wanted to trace his itinerary to Marx at the end of his life, *Tactics and Ethics* was chosen by him to represent one leg of this journey. The *Ontology of Social Being* became the culmination of that journey.

The inclusion of a short paper entitled *The Ontological Foundations of Human Thinking and Action* in the collection entitled *My Road to Marx*[4] testifies as to Lukács's intention and confirms also the validity of our argument in favor of the internal consistency of his life.

Chapter 3   PRAXIS AND THEORY: TACTICS AND ETHICS

Terrorism and the Notion of Freedom

Extremes have always attracted the attention of passersby as if the ordinary, everyday appearance of reality had lost its charm. It often seems that the indifference of ordinary people can be moved to compassion or action only by the violent expression of life and ideas. Even lovers of philosophy are subject to this human weakness, which we may call "early deafness." Perhaps some would find an excuse for it by saying that people are encouraged by the media, which have to draw profit from their sterile speculations. In view of this, how do we explain that one of Lukács's most exciting writings, *Tactics and Ethics,* received so little publicity, though it could have provoked great excitement?

Due to the scarcity of works on ethics in the Marxist tradition, especially works that take a clear and unambiguous stand on crucial moral issues, this short essay has a peculiar interest for us.

The facts speak for themselves. They draw our attention to both the necessity and the difficulty of such an undertaking. The necessity is clear to all; praxis needs rules so that it may not turn into tyranny. The difficulty is less evident to those who do not see the need to find a foundation in order to derive their rules from it. In ethics, the foundation is some kind of a *value.* We may then legitimately wonder what could have been the foundation of this first atempt, *Tactics and Ethics* — or, in our terminology, what theoretical foundation of praxis was developed in this early writing.

HISTORICAL BACKGROUND

Lukács wrote *Tactics and Ethics* when he joined the communist party some years before the Hungarian Communist Revolution of 1919. It contains, therefore, all the qualities, by which I mean, all the passions, of a neophyte who believes in what he says, and who has to convince himself first rather than others of the "tragic" beauty of a revolutionary commitment.

26

Furthermore, this essay, published in Hungarian while Lukács was commissar of education in the revolutionary government of Béla Kun, is also an essay on freedom. I would not call it an essay on political freedom only, because it touches on a series of problems more profound than the political liberty of a citizen or the collective liberty of groups, races, and nations.

THE PROBLEMATIC

Tactics and Ethics posits, with a brutal sincerity, the fundamental questions of human freedom: (1) What are the permissible means for the realization of an end, when this ideal is understood or believed to be a worthy end for action? (2) How far may an action on behalf of others, for the sake of others, be justified? (3) Is it legitimate for an individual to choose a way of life for others and in choosing it to interfere brutally with the lives of others who may happen to hinder its realization or happen simply to be in its way? (4) How is the value of life and sacrifice measured by freedom in the absolute sense? Here, I shall consider this last question only. I will not give a detailed analysis of Lukács's *Tactics and Ethics,* which bears the scars of the Hegelian philosophy and runs along the line of Marxist economic theories, because the conclusion — which is of interest to us — does not follow from the argument that precedes it. There is a leap between what may be called the historico-philosophical consciousness necessary for a correct political action and the question: Should one commit murder? I think no theoretician would ever dare to argue that the answer to this question is part of a historical analysis even if this analysis reveals some basic economic injustice that affects the life of human beings. To be more specific: I claim that however close the relation may be between economy and the life of individuals and nations, an act, in this case "murder," is not the necessary consequence of economic factors. An act of such importance cannot be considered without taking into account the question of freedom. Even if there are cases in which murder can be the direct result of a struggle for survival and placed on the level of an instinctive reaction to provocation, the terrorist's act is not one of them. The distinctive characteristic of the terrorist's act becomes evident from the context. Lukács raises the question whether the moment has arrived to enter the final stage of realization. This entry is similar to a *leap.* He also speaks of the arrival of a possibility which no science could properly determine. Hence, the terrorist's act is not only a conscious act, but a premeditated one, thus a genuinely free act originated in the volition of an individual.

Furthermore, in order for a murder to be a "murder," i.e., an act that transgresses the commandment not to kill, the murderer has to be conscious not only of the act, but also of the prohibition. Lukács insists on the fact that the terrorist is aware of his crime, that his awareness is a burden for him, but that this awareness must not stop him. This brings about the paradoxical situation in which he finds himself: he knows that he should not kill, but still he has to want the act. This paradox is the result of two irreconcilable commandments. The first says: do not kill; the second commands that murder be committed. In this way the paradox heightens the tension in the terrorist and makes his awareness of the crime even more acute. A crime of some sort becomes unavoidable: he has to commit either an act that transgresses the moral law or an act that betrays his political commitment.

THE PARADOX OF CRIME AND SACRIFICE

Having reached this point of tension, Lukács wants to show both the readiness and the reluctance of the terrorist in such a way that his act would be transformed into an ethical act. This would save the terrorist from being an *ordinary* murderer. Lukács has to find, then, the criterion of an acceptable act of terrorism (which means no less than the criterion of correct and incorrect murder). The solution flows from the insurmountable paradox that culminates in the self-sacrifice of the terrorist. The criterion of the correct and incorrect act of terrorism will be, in Lukács's terms, the *sacrifice*. The terrorist sacrifices his purity, his reputation, his life, for his friends and for the collectivity. To illustrate his theory, Lukács refers to Ropsin's novel, in which the author formulates the problem of terror in these terms: it is forbidden to kill, it is an unforgivable crime, but it is necessary and inevitable. The author sees in the sacrifice not the justification of the act, but its *ethical origin*.

The question arises: where do we find freedom in the context of this paradox? On the one hand, Lukács considers "the play of forces" as the condition of proper tactics, hence the condition of an act of terrorism. On the other hand, the real criterion of an act is the act itself, since no science can set the right time for the right action. Thus freedom is ground between the two stones of contradictory criteria, the *rational* and the *irrational*. Reason commands the act of terrorism in the name of the logic of history ("the decisive criterion of the socialist class struggle is the philosophy of history"), but this commandment remains only a theoretical necessity to which the individual has to adhere at a specific moment that he has to determine himself. If the moment is improperly chosen and the act fails to produce the right result, the act loses its ethical value, because according to Lukács, the criterion of right tactics is the right result.

What are the consequences of such a theory? Since the right result is the only criterion of right tactics — and vice versa: "the right tactics is already ethical in itself" — the *intention* to adhere to the theoretical necessity (or in

Kantian terms, to the categorical imperative) loses its ethical value.

Will the loss of the ethical value not bring with it the loss of the meaning of the sacrifice which is also the cornerstone of ethics for the terrorist? The conception of tactics *as* ethics constitutes, then, a fatal blow to *rationality,* which is always linked with human freedom.

Lukács's argument confirms this interpretation. We read in his essay that only the individual can ask for the reason or the "why" of his action; the collectivity relates only to tactics. If, on the other hand, correct tactics are also ethically correct, the individual has to disappear in favor of the collectivity, which follows by necessity the historico-logical development.

We may now ask: is there such a thing as *collective freedom?* The term itself seems to be inherently contradictory. To be part of a group, in submission to a collectivity, means the limitation of individual freedom. The limitation of individual responsibility means the limitation of the value of the human being as an individual. This implies the change in the connotation of murder. The terrorist, when he commits a murder, only removes a road block that is in the way of the well-being of the collectivity. Under these circumstances will the terrorist be able to retain the title "tragic hero" given to him by Lukács?

At the outset of our discussion we claimed that Lukács's endeavors can be brought under unity by a purpose he formulated thus: "to trace the direction of theoretical work for those who come after me. If I have succeeded in discovering the right method, then I may say that I lived well." This statement is a direct reference to the order of priorities regarding *theory* and *praxis,* and Lukács does not hesitate to illustrate it by alluding to the best Marxists, who "gave priority to science and theory." Stalin, of course, will not be counted among those classics. "Stalinism suffocated Marxist theory. He forged tactics and strategy from current political situations, then he did the worst thing one can do by dressing it in theoretical garments."[1]

These words, uttered by Lukács at the end of his life, must be taken as his "philosophical will," hence a sort of reminder of his intention in all his undertakings. This is what we read already in *Tactics and Ethics.* At the same time, giving theory priority over praxis, Lukács invites us to judge his own theorizing on praxis — in this case, terrorism — according to the standard advocated by himself: *the right method of theorizing.*

Now, if we are sure which is the right method of theorizing, we run again the risk of falling back to the old and insoluble issue of authenticity. To avoid this pitfall and to try to keep the debate on the level of *"theory"* we resort to our own criterion: internal consistency. Being confronted with a theoretical work, we shall apply what we called *second-level* internal consistency, namely, the internal consistency of a doctrine.

In the case of *Tactics and Ethics* and its aim to secure an ethical status for the terrorist and his act, this method will consist of testing the presuppositions of Lukács that are meant to establish the *autonomy* of an act and its value, using the criterion of *sacrifice,* which transforms the terrorist into a *tragic hero.*

Presenting the terrorist as a tragic hero is possible only in an ethical order whose commandments are not subject to historical becoming. But Lukács defines the proper ethical act as depending on the recognition of a given historico-philosophical situation. In this sense, the ethical commandment is subject to historical becoming in the Marxian sense, and with it, the individual's freedom will be subject to this historico-philosophical necessity. In other words, if the truth expressed by the commandment becomes historical, the individual's freedom will be swallowed by historical necessity and the "tragic situation" of the terrorist will mark only a stage of the *mediation* between an earlier and a later historical moment. Moreover, with the increase of necessity goes the decrease of liberty.

Lukács's dramatic presentation of the terrorist's sacrifice (and also Rapsin's hero) is borrowed from the Christian tradition and recalls the paradox of faith in Kierkegaard's *Fear and Trembling.* (Lukács states elsewhere that Kierkegaard played an important role in his intellectual development while he was in Heidelberg and that he even intended to write an essay on the latter's critique of Hegel's philosophy.)

It is worth noticing tht Lukács quotes from Hebbel's *Judith* to support his argument. In this context, not crime, but *sin,* a Judeo-Christian concept, is employed to heighten the paradox, and with it the terrorist's tragic sacrifice. Lukács even distorts the quotation to suit his purpose. He writes: "to express this sense of the most profound human tragedy in the incomparably beautiful words of Hebbel's *Judith:* "Even if God had placed sin between me and the deed enjoined upon me, who am I to escape it?" Judith's actual words are: "If You [God] had placed sin between me and my deed, who am I to quarrel about it with You and to escape form You?"[2]

The comparison between these two quotations reveals the principle that we want to oppose to Lukács's interpretation of tragedy. There are tragedies that may involve mankind as a whole, but there is a tragic hero only if a man has to make a free choice between two orders of ethics taken as equally *absolute.* Hebbel's Judith is fighting with *God,* not with *history.* She is caught between two commandments that come from an equally absolute source. This is paradoxical, incomprehensible, and therefore tragic, if Judith believes in God. The evaluation of her act depends entirely on the absolute commandments and not on the actual success or failure of her deed in the light of *history.* Tension is at its peak only under these circumstances, because freedom is also an absolute. Disobedience to a relative command is merely relative disobedience.

As Lukács pleads the case of the terrorist, he relies on two different points of view, two different orders of ethics and therefore two different kinds of freedom—the individual and the collective—out of which he chooses the collective as being the determining factor. Hence the ethical orders found in Lukács's argument are of unequal value, as measured by freedom. The confrontation of the two orders could produce a tension only if the two kinds of freedom had been kept on the same level of importance. We doubt, therefore, that Lukács has succeeded in securing for the terrorist the title of "tragic hero" even on the ground of his own principles, because by placing his hero under "conditional" laws he has impaired the freedom of his hero and in so doing, lowered the tension of the tragic situation. Thus, he has also impaired his basic criterion of values: *sacrifice.*

We may conclude that Lukács's insistence on the sacrifice as criterion of value for the terrorist's act makes sense only in an ethical system that is based on absolute ethical laws (do not kill; love your neighbor; or the categorical imperative) that suffer no exceptions.

Lukács considered writing a Marxist ethics at the end of his life, but abandoned it in favor of an ontology, because he realized that ethics requires ontological foundations, or, put differently, that *praxis* demands a *theoretical foundation.* We should then find an answer to the question of freedom in this later work. Alas, our expectations are not fulfilled. In a paper prepared for the Fourteenth International Congress of Philosophy held in Vienna in 1968 Lukács presents an overall view of his project. But we find very little on freedom that could help us to elucidate our problems. What is found in this little work and in the *Ontology* on freedom has to be reconstrued, along with those presuppositions (or principles) that condition freedom. Among them we can list the *origin* of consciousness, *Widerspiegelung* ("reflection"), and the dialectic of nature. As we mentioned earlier, any act may have at its origin a reason, but rationality means a *consistency* among reasons. Only when the latter criterion is fulfilled is it possible to speak of a theory.

We must state, then, that with the exception of vague allusions to freedom, Lukács avoided the problem. Could this reluctance to take up formally the question of freedom be the cause of his failure to establish a Marxist ethics?

There is yet another question: if the foundation of ethics is a value of some kind, should freedom not be counted among those values?

We may sum up the argument as follows: the ethical value of an act of terrorism, defined by Lukács as self-sacrifice, and the idea of the terrorist as tragic hero, are inconceivable for a Marxist, because neither the commandment nor freedom are taken as absolute, but only as relative to a situation, and as dependent on a result. So, to make of his terrorist a tragic hero, Lukács had to borrow from Christian tradition the notion of sin, freedom, and paradox.

THEORY AS INTELLECTUAL HONESTY

This early writing stands out among Lukács's work as a memorable effort to give Marxism a theoretical foundation. Of course, Novack could interject that Lukács was influenced during his early years as a Marxist by the extreme left anarchist movement: that would rule out his being a Marxist. Lukács, who spoke of this period of his intellectual and political development, has not mentioned names that could suggest such an influence. Novack's suggestion is not likely to be correct for another reason. This was also a period in Lukács's life when he envisaged becoming engaged in academic activities — see his application for a teaching position at the University of Heidelberg. But even if Novack were right, the thesis holds that Lukács, as an intellectual, sought in all practical engagement the reason that justified commitment.

However, it is certainly also true about this stage of Lukács's Marxism that it aspired towards a total commitment, which drew forth every consequence of praxis including the ultimate one, *terrorism*. Is it not to Lukács's credit that he understood the essence of a political praxis with its inevitable *historical* consequences, rather than indulging in the sort of one-sided, comfortable, academic Marxism engaged in by innumerable Western intellectuals who systematically rule out the possibility of violence in Marxist political praxis? Only this total commitment leading to its ultimate consequences could put the question of tactics and ethics in its most acute form and demand an answer.

It is obvious also that Lukács *had to find* the answer where it was possible to find it, and this led inevitably beyond Marxism in its historical form. The notions of murder and of transgression of the commandment have become logical necessities in the rational interpretation of the terrorist's act. And Marxism, in building an ethics, has no choice but to be rational, because only such an ethics is compatible with its overall ambition, namely to be a *scientific ideology*. Therefore, it is all the more stunning to find in this context the notion of sacrifice, referring here to the sacrifice of one's *purity* (which, like *sin*, is undoubtedly a religious term).

Furthermore, let us not forget the underlying or implicit need for a criterion, without which it would have been impossible to tell right from wrong. In this respect Lukács is almost unique in the Marxist camp, for he understood very early the importance of theory in the elaboration of an *authentic* Marxist praxis. If Lukács acquired this manner of reasoning from

Hegel, should he be blamed for it? Only reasoning according to principles carries within itself the test of consistency. It is such reasoning that led Lukács to the conception of his *Ontology* as a universal science of being. Ideologies in general (and Marxism is no exception) suffer from the practice of elevating particular examples to the rank of universality.[3] Such a practice has, from the ethical point of view, disastrous consequences. It is interesting to note that Lukács was aware of this shortcoming of praxis soon after he committed himself to enter the communist party. Lukács had to borrow notions otherwise unwarranted by the teaching of dialectical materialism in his attempt to secure the internal consistency of his theory. We may safely state that even if the idea of sin may be omitted from his account as unnecessary, it is not so with the idea of freedom.

* * *

Tactics and Ethics opens and closes quickly an era in Lukács's life; it opens the way to a political commitment that culminates in his participation in the short-lived communist revolution of 1919 in Hungary; the failure of this revolution marks at the same time the end of this kind of commitment. This does not mean that Lukács has withdrawn from politics, but it somehow cancels short-range *political praxis* that could have lead to immediate or direct involvement. Then how is it that his theoretical activity, which surfaces most eloquently in his essays published in *History and Class Consciousness,* provoked such a violent reaction on the part of the official party stand? The answer is probably that theory was taken seriously at that time; and the ambition to establish the official interpretation of Marx, and after this the criterion of authentic Marxism, was in the foreground of the feverish political discussions. Since nobody had tried seriously, i.e., philosophically, to give praxis a theoretical foundation, the enterprise was judged from vague ideological points of view whose consistency had so far not been tested. Such was, for example Engels's dialectic of nature. For Lukács, those years offered innumerable challenges. There were also occasional digressions from the task he had set himself. Though it may seem paradoxical, he himself understood this only in retrospect. It is not unusual that writers, politicians, and philosophers become conscious of the consistency of their own striving only at a later date. Did not Balzac, halfway through his work, discover that he was writing "la comédie humaine"? The same is true for Lukács. The internal consistency of which I made mention and which I put forward as the measure of authenticity for the life of Lukács became evident only later in Lukács's career, and for obvious reasons. It was in retrospect that Lukács could contemplate his success or failure in interpreting social and cultural phenomena. He could write only in retrospect his *Road to Marx* and see a continuous thread running through his whole enterprise.

Thus, we do not force Lukács into an artificial or scholarly straight-jacket. Lukács confirmed, first unconsciously, then consciously, his own position: this he named at a later stage of his life "Marxist theory," or the extension and continuation of Marx.[4] Hence, we will leap over the period when Lukács himself was not fully aware of his undertaking. When examining the production of this intermediate period, it would appear that the 1960s brought to light in Lukács what he later considered, shortly before his death, to have been the purpose of his life.

If it is hazardous to speculate on his reasons for writing most of the books and essays that belong to this period, including his work on existentialism (Sartre, Heidegger, and Nietzsche) — which Lucien Goldmann, one of his admirers, brushed completely aside in favor of his early works, up to 1923 — it is not meaningless to reflect upon the notions that governed his interpretation in these works when we consider what happened to these notions *(Widerspiegelung,* dialectic of nature, freedom, ontology) in his last work, the *Ontology,* which we have called his *philosophical autobiography* and also his last and irrevocable *autocriticism.*

Details of a praxis acquire new importance in the light of a theory; and ontology is theory on the highest level. One could even say that it is the swan song of philosophy and that only the best specimens of this race of thinkers should venture to take part in the audition. Not everyone who is about to die sings so beautifully that posterity will remember them for it. Nevertheless, writings in this category have their importance regardless of the success or failure of this venture. After all, ontology is a pure theory, even when it originates in paraxis, as is the case with Lukács. This is evident from his original intent, which was to write an ethics for Marxism. As a pure theory, ontology becomes the test for the *internal consistency* of both theory and praxis. Our interest in Lukács's theoretical venture centers on this point.

Regardless of the criticism a leap over a long period of literary and philosophical writing may provoke, the internal logic of our approach requires us to go from *Tactics and Ethics* to the *Ontology.* After all, the preoccupation of both is ethics, i.e., praxis viewed from the angle of theory. If one wished to force generalization just a little, one could affirm that *Tactics and Ethics* foreshadows the *Ontology* because in it duty is based on an ontological structure, viz., the exigencies of sociohistorical development. Duty, in this case, is an objective commandment, almost a categorical imperative for one who is able to understand the exigencies that surface in history. The necessity of an ontological structure becomes even more evident when the aim is not only political tactics, but the elaboration of a general ethics.

Chapter 4   Theory of Praxis: The *Ontology*

Even the best intention to be fair or impartial when writing on such a controversial figure as Lukács may fail on the stumbling block of the distrust of those readers who seem to detect in every non-Marxist interpretation an ideological bias. Regardless of their suspicion, I am determined to pursue this task of elucidating, on the basis of the *Ontology,* Lukács's ultimate position on the most fundamental issues of Marxism. There is no doubt that the reconciliation of *theory* and *praxis* could be named as the thorniest issue in Marxist philosophy or ideology.

Ideology vs Ontology

Announcing the problem as it is formulated in the title would be sufficient to arouse a heated debate on the subject, because the defender of Marx would consider this approach as revealing the usual bourgeois bias. Marxism conceived in its orthodox form would not recognize the independent existence of "philosophy"; therefore it could not recognize the independent existence of ontology either. This fact alone supports the novelty of Lukács's undertaking and, at the same time, increases the difficulty of our own task, namely, to define, at least for the purpose of our investigations, the meaning of those terms.

If the definition of ideology is relatively easy according to orthodox Marxism, with the change of times, the numerous interpretations of Marx's teaching, and especially the effort of "progressive" Marxists who labor hard to make Marxism "philosophically" acceptable, a uniform answer to the question is now almost impossible. We have to be satisfied, therefore, with the general idea of ideology, or, if it is permitted to use a non-Marxist terminology, the essence of ideology. Then we may disregard the change in the vocabulary and accept both Marxist ideology and Marxist philosophy as equally meaningful terms, since the essence of the Marxist notion of philosophy and ideology will be the determining factor in our discussion.

The first indication of what ideology is, according to Marx, is found in the well-known statement of his eleventh thesis on Feuerbach: "Philosophers have only interpreted the world in various ways, the point is to change it." The interpretation of the world was taken by Marx for the justification of the existing order of things, since he considered this interpretation as the product of socioeconomic causes. Hence, philosophy, along with religion, has become false ideology or false consciousness, having as its aim the perpetuation of a world order.[1] I do not wish to claim that this view still prevails unchanged in all Marxist circles, but it was certainly the opinion of the Russian delegate to the fourteenth International Congress of Philosophy (Vienna, 1968). In his paper on "Philosophy and Ideology" he defines "ideology" as the combination of certain ideas. Its main characteristics are inevitably superstructured over society's natural life in the form of political, legal, religious, ethical, and philosophical views.[2] Since philosophy is superstructured and only part of an ideology, this implies that neither philosophy nor ontology is an independent discipline.

If we ask how Marxism is defined by the same Marxist, the answer will be: "Marxism presents a consistently scientific ideology—a complete and regular system of philosophical, economical, social and political views."[3] If we compare these formulations of ideology to the one we find in Herder's *Kleines philosophisches Wörterbuch,* we notice that it is a quite accurate rendering of what Marxist thinkers thought of ideology: "It is a term used in reflection of the economic conditions of a class."[4] The superiority of Marxism would be, according to its own definition, the "consistent" scientific view, which guarantees the independence of this ideology from the economic conditions of a class.

Regardless of the usage of the terms "philosophy" and "ideology" by contemporary Marxist "philosophers," philosophy and ideology in their own definition will always imply a "scientific knowledge" as an essential characteristic. Gadamer's and Ricoeur's intervention in the recent debates on ideology is a protest against the scientific arrogance of the Frankfurt School and of Althusser.[5]

Now, whether Marxism would like to be a scientific ideology or a philosophy attributing to its own method a scientific value, it is still to be proven if strict scientific knowledge is possible to achieve in the field of philosophy and the social sciences. Marxist ideology, then, is a world view (*Weltanschauung*), or an interpretation of social, economic, and cultural phenomena, which is dependent on Marx's basic presupposition as explanatory principle—the economic condition of the proletariat or the class struggle.

My definitiion of ideology, then, questions not only the scientific objectivity of Marxism, but also its freedom to think otherwise. The ground for this opinion is found also in Marx's elevent thesis on Feuerbach: ". . . the point is to change the world." Thinking, then, should go along the line of the proposed change. Therefore, Marxism in any form—whether we call it ideology or philosophy—is subservient to Marx's political doctrines, i.e., subservient to praxis. In other terms, Marx's philosophy leaves little room for the questioning of the validity of praxis.

I would like to note here that Lukács's use of the term "Ideology" in his paper on ontology, which is a kind of summary of his major work, *The Ontology of Social Being,* is rather inconsistent. When he alludes to ideologies he seems to mean false consciousness (e.g., magic, religion). At other places, he associates ideology with tendencies that tackle concrete problems (e.g., as the human species endeavors to assert its specific nature). Then, in the same "Vienna Paper,"[6] he attributes to "great philosophy and great art" and to the exemplary behavior of great men of action the merit of preparing the realm of freedom for man. (VP, pp. 154; 163.)

Even if we assume an irreconcilable antagonism between the two views, namely the Marxist and non-Marxist definitions of philosophy, this does not exclude the possibility of discussing this topic. As Gadamer says, there are no terms, but only connotations of a term, hence we will have a basis for discussion.[7] I would define philosophy as a discipline which is free, under any social, political, economic, or cultural circumstances, to reconsider its own presuppositions and revise its interpretation of the world and all phenomena in the world.[8]

If the definition of ideology and philosophy was relatively easy and could probably serve, even if some amendments were needed, for the basis of discussion, the definition of ontology raises serious problems. Nevertheless, the definition of ontology is imperative if we want to invite Lukács's *Ontology* to answer our questions, namely, whether it is an ontology or simply another form of ideology.

There is an ontology associated with metaphysics (either Platonic or Aristotelian), which continued to exist and develop all through the Middle Ages. Its main characteristics are: causality and the absolute (in some form). Hegel's ontology is a distant echo of this system because of the notion of the absolute and the dialectical movement. As opposed to these, we have the phenomenological ontologies, one of them being the *Fundamentalontologie* of Heidegger. I would call them *descriptive ontologies.*[9]

Having listed the contradictory characteristics of two great categories of ontology, can we still claim that it is possible to reach an agreement on the essentials and define, for the purpose of our discussion, what we understand by ontology? We should be able to find the characteristics that are common to all ontologies in order to elucidate the purpose of ontological speculations. Aristotle writes: "there is a science which takes up the theory of being as being and of what 'to be' means taken by itself" *(Metaph.* 4, 1)." However, it soon appears that "being" has several meanings, but that they all have central reference to "some one nature" *(Metaph.* 4, 2), which suggests not merely the classification of beings *(onta),* but also the degrees of being, namely, an ontological scale. I would even suggest a term, which is uncommon in ontologies but which correctly denotes this additional meaning; that is, an ontological scale of values. Thus, what appears at first sight to be an objective science similar to logic or mathematics, the theory of "being as being," which investigates the most general characteristics of being, moves towards qualitative differentiation. (What logician could ever include in the same equation the being of essence and of accident, or being *in potentia* and being *in actu*?)

One may object that what is true for Aristotle's metaphysics would not apply to Husserl's ontology. Does not Husserl's reduction present a scheme of beings which, in Max Scheler's ontology, becomes the foundation of values? In Heidegger's descriptive ontology this scheme runs from concealment to revelation of Being (Sein); in existentialism, from inauthentic to authentic existence. Although there is a radical change in the the principle of explanation, Aristotelian (and of course Platonic) and phenomenological ontologies contain — at least implicitly — a *qualitative* element as their common and distinctive characteristic.[10]

Since we are convinced that no common denominator of science and philosophy will ever be found — even Nicolai Hartmann's ontology (which comes closest to a scientific ontology) discounts this eventuality — our position on ontology should not surprise anyone. Did Heidegger not receive his metaphysical training from Brentano, whose book on the *Multiple Significance of Being in Aristotle* he read and reread several times?

There is another common characteristic of ontology, which I would call the metaphysical element. Metaphysics in the sense of *philosophia prima* undertakes the difficult task of explaining "being as being," which leads to the unification of phenomena under some basic principles.[11] Heidegger expresses his amazement at the end of his *Was ist Metaphysik?* in these terms: "How is it that instead of nothing there is something?" We know that Plato wrote the *Timaeus* to answer this question, and we also know that Aristotle avoided it by taking the world as eternal; instead he labored to explain change, and the laws or principles that explain change became the unifying principle of his ontology. Hegel's *Phänomenologie des Geistes* is construed on four premises, says Kojève, the Marxist interpreter of Hegel: "When we accept these four premises we understand the possibility of historical process, also history which is — on the whole — the history of struggle and work, that finally surface in the Napoleonic wars; and we understand the table on which Hegel wrote his *Phänomenologie des Geistes* in order to understand these wars and this table."[12]

In other words, the four premises explain everything. We may single out any one of these ontologies and our findings will be the same: ontological explanation is not based on scientific laws or a priori principles.

We may now conclude that the unifying principles of an ontology must be nonscientific in order to allow for a scale of being, or even, as we stated earlier, for a scale of values. Indiscriminate uniformity, the necessary condition for the mathematization of nature (cf. Descartes's *res extensa*), cannot explain the degrees of being based on "some one nature" *(Metaph., 4, 2, 1002a)*. This is the reason why we have to reject both positivist metaphysics and scientific ontology. Now the question is: to which one of these ontologies did Lukács commit himself, since he found no example to follow in the Marxist tradition? One thing appears certain: Lukács rejected outright the superior types of beings; it is obvious. In spite of this, Lukács's ontology seeks to accommodate qualitative differences; therefore it will have some similarity with the ontologies we have described. Naturally this similarity *in principle* does not exclude Lukács's vehement attacks on almost every type of ontology.

A philosophy oriented towards *praxis* has difficulty in adjusting itself to philosophy proper or to ontology. As a *praxis,* a philosophy moves towards its realization, and it may revise, stage after stage, or according to given circumstances, the rules of the game. It is possible to reject a formula after it has been proven inefficient. But an ontology is a pure theory and for this reason it acquires an independence even in the philosophy of praxis, and in this way it becomes its own measure, or, if we use the criterion Whitehead set for the evaluation of metaphysics, we say that the success of an ontology depends on its applicability.[13] It is obvious that applicability does not mean here praxis, but applicability to all phenomena. While the dialectics of praxis is moving towards the realization of an objective, in ontology, we may say, Marxism returns towards itself. Hence ontology, being a pure theory, is a test of consistency.

We wonder whether Lukács realized the hazards of his undertakings. He wanted to be a Marxist scientist (according to the definition of Marxism), but ontology is not a science (in the modern sense of this term) and Lukács would agree with us. Does he not reject logic and positivism as useless sciences when they come to grips with the problem of being? Then one may foresee that ontology will be a test, not only of Marxism, but Lukács's own fidelity to Marx. Finally, this will be a fidelity revised according to the necessities of ontology, hence a fidelity that is symbolic rather than real.

The Birth of the *Ontology*

If we search for the birth of the *Ontology* in Lukács's works, or if we attempt to unveil through the examination of earlier works the origin of this very last undertaking, our search can produce some result only if we look at Lukács's theoretical activity in retrospect, namely, from the point of view of the *Ontology*, whose origin we are investigating. This method looks paradoxical, for, one wonders, had Lukács himself a clear idea about what ontology meant? or was it that his successive attempts to provide a theoretical basis for Marxism led him, without his knowledge, to this "science," so alien to the original intent of Marx himself? Of course, we refer here to Marx's eleventh thesis on Feuerbach, since undoubtedly the first part of this thesis — the interpretation of the world — could be taken, in the broad sense of the term, for the definition and also the negation of ontology. Then, does it not sound somewhat bizarre that the first sentence of the Prolegomena to Lukács's *Ontology* reads as follows: "Nobody was more concerned with an overall view of the ontology of social being than Marx"? Thus, Lukács refers to the classics of Marxism, who, in his opinion, have taken a "concrete" stand on this issue, to justify this rather bold statement. I refrain here from pronouncing judgment on the success or failure of Lukács in this particular undertaking. The issue at stake is now the *origin* of the *Ontology* and its nature. By "nature" I mean the distincitve characteristics of this philosophical discipline, and must raise the issue whether Lukács was led to its discovery by the necessity of its permanent characteristics, in which case he would have had little success adopting it to Marxist philosophy; or is ontology Lukács's invention, at least the way he means it, in which case he could accommodate the classics of Marxist philosophy in the framework of this philosophical discipline?

We have seen that in traditional philosophy, ontology is the science of being. Aristotle raised the question in terms of his metaphysics, when he asked, "What is being?" or, more exactly, "What is primary being?" This question itself suggests already that ontology becomes, by necessity, a *systematic* investigation of "being" and this implies the *interconnection of principles* in the elaboration of ontology. In such a way all beings are also interconnected, that is, interdependent. We are conscious that this statement is valid only in the context of an ontology based on *causality* and held together by a universal *teleology*. "Descriptive ontologies" of the phenomenological method follow other rules. Now, since Lukács writes the "Ontology of *Social* Being," he cannot neglect to answer the deeper question, "What is being?" These questions, due to the interconnectedness of ontological issues, will force him in turn, to deal with the problems of teleology and freedom. This is the law of internal consistency. We find therefore, as we mentioned earlier, this double exigency checking each other's authenticity, namely the internal consistency of a life and the internal consistency of a theory that commands the realizations of a life.

Now, is it conceivable that Lukács can, on his own, change the nature of ontology in such a way that his *Ontology of Social Being* could do without some of the characteristics of a general ontology; for example, the interconnectedness or unity of interpretation; or, more exactly, could the problem of social being supercede the more fundamental issues "What is being?", "What is an individual being?"; or "What is man?" If these problems are related in such a way that the question "What is being?" leads necessarily to "What is primary being?", the internal consistency of the doctrine will demand the elaboration of these issues in taking into account the principle of relatedness.

When examining the last work of Lukács, his *Ontology,* we do not fail to notice that Lukács was driven by the logic intrinsic to this discipline to attempt an elaboration similar to the traditional model. Hence, ontology imposes itself not only on anyone who sets as his aim the interpretation of the world, but also on those who seek an interpretation of praxis. Marxist thinkers before Lukács failed to notice, or if they did, tried to avoid stressing, the fact that one has to justify praxis in order to make it rational. Once it is recognized, the interpretation of the world becomes unavoidable.

The Genesis of the *Ontology*

Lukács has left approximately two thousand pages of manuscript bearing the general title *Zur Ontologie des gesellschaftlichen Seins,* which we can translate: *The Ontology of Social Being,* or, taking into consideration the preposition *"zur,"* we may find a more modest title — *Contributions to the Ontology of Social Being."*

The lengthy *Ontology* is full of digressions, repetitions, and ambiguities, and its two thousand pages turn away most readers. The innumerable detours it takes for Lukács to come to grips with his problems also reduces the impact of this work on current Marxist thinking. This situation will remain unchanged for a long time unless non-Marxist thinkers discover in the novelty of the ontological method in Marxism an attempt to secure a solid theoretical foundation for praxis. Indeed, the *Ontology* will become the greatest embarrassment for Marxism from the moment it is taken seriously by Marxists. But this moment may be far off.

The *Ontology* testifies to the ultimate effort of a Marxist thinker to sort out the principles underlying social and economic praxis and to found the latter on a system of interlocked causes that would account for all phenomena beginning with the most important among them, namely social being, which starts with the emergence of man. It is in the *Ontology* that Lukács intends to fulfill his commitment to an ideal he set for himself: to give a theoretical foundation to Marxism and to *continue* Marx in order to make his teaching fit to respond to the new problems that emerge with new circumstances.[14]

If we wanted to speculate on the lack of success of this work in spite of its novelty, we would not be far from the truth in affirming that nowadays such an undertaking is as alien to non-Marxist thinkers as to Marxist theoreticians. Ontology, in the *traditional sense,* (and this is how Lukács conceived it), is uncommon nowadays in philosophical literature for the following reason: ontology, hence the *science of being,* is synonmous with metaphysics. It is obvious that Lukács would not have called his work a metaphysics after the well-known and devastating criticism of Hume and Kant. Nevertheless, his ontology falls into the category of traditional ontologies, meaning that the principles which explain the emergence and existence of beings are also the criteria of their *proper* way of existing. Ontology in this sense provides the *standards* not only for the existence, but also for the functioning of being, in Lukács's case, of social being. Expressing this in the term we have already proposed, ontology is *"the theory of praxis."* This view is confirmed by Lukács when he writes: *"Keine Ethik ohne Ontologie."* This sentence is found among the notes he prepared for his Marxist ethics.[15] Now, it is obvious that ethics needs standards to determine actions and to formulate its commandments. Undoubtedly, Lukács meant to write the *Ontology* to spell out those standards. It is, then, confirmed that *Tactics and Ethics* can be taken as a sort of prolegomena to his *Ontology* according to its *intent* and *method.*

Although Lukács insists on his fidelity to Marx and to materialist principles and although he affirms Marx's great insight, claiming that we find already in his writing the foundations of an ontology, it is a puzzling question whether he had no other models than Marx to write his *Ontology.* One thing is certain: he did not find the term in Marx or any other Marxist sources. What is also amazing for a Marxist is the connection of ethics and ontology. This connection only exists in classical and medieval philosophy. If Garaudy could have glanced into the *Ontology* of Lukács, perhaps he would not have written, or at least not in the same way, his *Marxism in the Twentieth Century.* It would also have helped Lucien Goldmann in his venture to compare Heidegger to Lukács. The end result would have been different from what we find in his book *Lukács and Heidegger.*[16]

The *Ontology* is now a fact, since it is written. But its sources are unknown or remain enigmatic. That Lukács used Nicolai Hartmann's model may be suggested by circumstances and some chapters of the *Ontology.* Nevertheless, it does not solve the enigma why *"Keine Ethik ohne Ontologie"*?[17]

We must believe Lukács when he says that after the aesthetics he wanted to write an ethics for Marxism. But while trying to elaborate his plan he ran into difficulties that made him realize that there is "no ethics without ontology." One is rightly puzzled about this statement and the all-important question arises: how did Lukács find his way from ethics to ontology?

Another curious question also remains unanswered: why did Lukács read, during the years of reflection prior to writing the *Ontology,* almost all the important theologians of the Middle Ages and of our times, from the works of St. Augustine and Thomas Aquinas to the *Dogmatics* of Karl Barth?[18] One may say that Lukács was inquisitive and read all sorts of books. But why did he stuff his envelopes with notes on theologians while preparing his work on ethics? If the maxim *"No ethics without ontology"* applies anywhere, it applies in theology. Whatever theology it may be, the moment the creation of the world is assumed and attributed to God, the purposiveness of all creatures somehow follows form the intention of the maker. Thus, St. Augustine writes in the *Confessions:* "Fecisti nos ad te . . ." ("You have made us for yourself. . .").[19] This sentence constitutes the ontological foundation of morals: from God, back to God.

Of course, theology is not ontology, but it does define what a man is, what he should do, and what he can hope for. This means that theology in its own way covers all domains of ontology. Therefore, why not venture that theology, rather than Hartmann, supplied Lukács with the idea of writing an ontology on which to found ethics? Theology is, in its own way, the *theory of praxis,* and, one must add, not only of religious praxis, since out of theology arises a general moral philosophy encompassing both private and public life.

On this ground would it not be reasonable to conjecture that Hartmann became the model for *Ontology* only after the idea of writing such a work was born in the mind of Lukács? Once the decision was made, it was not difficult to trace the history of this science, which Lukács has done in the first, historical, part of his *Ontology.* To this part belongs what he calls *"Die gegenwärtige Problemlage"* ("The present state of the problem [of Ontology]") — existentialism, positivism, Hartmann, Hegel, and Marx. Then came the theoretical part: labor, alienation, reproduction, and ideology.

The *Ontology:* A Posthumous Work

According to statements made by Lukács to friends and journalists, this work had started in the 1960s. We know that it was completed, or almost completed, before his death. I can confirm this, having examined the original manuscript of the *Ontology.* (I mention the following as a *fait divers:* Lukács wrote his text on the back of letters received during the mid 1960s from the Hungarian Academy of Sciences and from other administrative agencies.) However, to what extent the *Ontology* was completed to Lukács's satisfaction is hard to tell.

Although we read in the published part of the original text by Luchterhand that the text is published after the manuscript and authorized by

Lukács,[20] we find a somewhat different story in the preface to *Utam Marxhoz* *"My Road to Marx,"* written in 1969, shortly before Lukács's death.

Lukács writes there: "Although it sounds paradoxical, now when I am over 80, I am about to write my most important work."[21] He became conscious, he says, of the important role of a new ontology in the current revival of Marxism. Does it mean that Marxism in its old form did not satisfy him any more, and, when he was more than eighty, he wanted to start everything anew and different? Lukács himself claims to remain faithful to his master. Nevertheless, we may safely say that he noticed serious lacunae in the philosophy of Marxism.

Considering the circumstances that led to the conception and realization of a work on ontology, the question naturally arises: was Lukács able to complete his *Ontology* or has he left only the broken pieces of a great monument? Again, in the preface of *Utam Marxhoz,* Lukács alludes to his latest work and notes that he was not satisfied with it and could not let it out of his hands because it needed revision. Did he really have the time? The preface is dated October 1969, and Lukács died in June 1971. However, his publisher, Luchterhand, announced the projected publication of the *Ontology* as volumes 13 and 14 of Lukács's *Complete Works.* So far, Luchterhand has published separately three small volumes taken out of *Zur Ontologie des gesellschaftlichen Seins* (*"The Ontology of Social Being"*): *Hegels falsche und echte Ontologie* (*"Hegel's False and True Ontology"*); *Die ontologieschen Grundprinzipien von Marx* (*"The Fundamental Ontological Principles of Marx"*) and *Die Arbeit* (*"Labor"*).

Lukács's Apprenticeship in Ontology

We have credited Lukács with the merit of rediscovering the usefulness of ontology, and, what is even more surprising, ontology for Marxism; nevertheless, in the construction of this science Lukács had so many illustrious predecessors that it was impossible for him to be innovative. However, since earlier ontologies achieved *internal consistency* at the cost of appearing unscientific, taking into their system ideas that were borrowed either from religion (e.g., the creation of the world by God), or from philosophy (a universal teleology), Lukács could not follow their examples uncritically. This is why he turned to a contemporary thinker, Nicolai Hartmann, who tried to avoid those mistakes and came close to constructing an ontology that, with some amendments, could have become a model for Lukács.

What was it in Hartmann's work that made Lukács value it? First of all, Hartmann's *realism* and his attempt to cover the *totality of beings* without reference to the then-dominant view of Kantianism, the division of the world into *phenomena* and *things in themselves.*[22] Being a *realism,* this ontology relied on *itself:* it did not borrow religious problems from earlier systems, nor was it the end result of a metaphysics. Moreover, it did not give in to contemporary positivism, on the contrary, it tried to extend the domination of philosophy over the sciences (p. 186). Hence, this ontology was not a form of epistemology on the model of positivism. "Erkenntnis gibt es nur von dem, was erst einmal 'ist' " ("There is knowledge only of that which already "exists" "), writes Lukács after Hartman. Therefore, Hartmann makes the distinction between ontological and epistemological principles. Furthermore, faithful to his "realism," his ontological principles originate in reality rather than being superimposed on reality from above. This method leads to an ontology that grows from its foundation, from things, that is, "from below" ("*von unten*"), thus avoiding any deductive method (p. 177).

One could, says Lukács, sum up Hartmann's merits in this sentence: his ontology is based on phenomena and not on hypotheses (p. 177).

But Hartmann had some serious shortcomings, and for this reason Lukács accepted his ontology only with amendments. Lukács's most serious objection concerns the neglect of *genesis* in Hartmann's system; Lukács attributes to this notion a great importance in the intepretation of the emergence of new categories. Lukács is convinced that Hartmann's most significant contribution could have been an emphasis on *genesis,* which was neglected by the old types of ontologies.

We have stated earlier that ontology is a kind of autocriticism, a test of the internal consistency of a system, and Hartmann's ontology is no exception to this rule. Seeing Lukács's serious objection to Hartmann, we may wonder whether Lukács correctly understood this law of internal consistency and whether he really wished to be as *objective* (impartial) as he tried to seem.

Marxist ontology definitely needs the notion of *genesis.* Is dialectical materialism not a form of genesis? On the other hand, we shall see, when criticizing Hartmann, what price is paid, in the form of concessions to the much criticized "old types" of ontologies, when Lukács adds the idea of genesis.

First, let us determine if Lukács is right in citing the neglect of *genesis* as a serious shortcoming in Hartmann's ontology.

Following, as before, the golden rule of *internal consistency,* do we not have to find an excuse for Hartmann's avoidance of the idea of genesis? Does the exclusion of genesis not fall in line with his reluctance to admit teleology into his system, especially the type that originates in some form of creation? Universal teleology is rejected by Hartmann, but has to be included in Lukács's ontology, because Marxist ontology needs teleology along with genesis to explain the emergence of phenomena. Lukács has to *import* them from *outside,* through *intuition,* since they cannot be deduced from phenomena alone. Genesis and its laws are similar in nature to the laws of evolution, which are equally intuited in reality. Their validity is tested through application. On Lukács's part it is only wishful thinking to consider them objective, i.e., infallible scientific laws. Genesis, whether he likes it or not, is a *metaphysical* law. We have to go to Hartmann's defense on this issue, because at the outset Hartmann made it clear that: "Dieses bunte Durcheinander von Sinnvollem und Sinnwidrigem braucht durchaus nicht teleologisch gedeutet zu werden; es ist ja in ihm keinerlei vorgezeichnete Richtung" ("This mixture of the meaningful and the paradoxical does not need at all to be explained with the help of teleology; there is no way to find in them a definite direction").[23]

If ontology is, as we have affirmed, the test of the *internal consistency* of a doctrine, Lukács had better stay with a kind of ontology that implies a teleology. If Hartmann's merit is to have based his ontology on *phenomena* and not on *hypotheses,* Lukács should have foreseen that the negation of teleology ("vorgezeichnete Richtung") and the neglect of the notion of *genesis* were integral parts of Hartmann's doctrine. Both were indeed the logical implications of his basic presupposition, which Lukács noted correctly: to grasp the phenomena *without* borrowing forms, contents, tendencies, and structures that are not inherent in the characteristics of phenomena. This will enable Hartmann, writes Lukács, to avoid both all philosophical half-solutions and also the opposition of idealism and realism (p. 179). On the other hand, Lukács failed to see that what constitutes Hartmann's merit in Lukács's own eyes, namely the *independence* of the ontology from the so-called philosophical half-solutions that are based on notions borrowed from traditional ontologies, will also exclude from Hartmann's system the notion that Lukács needs most, the notion of *genesis.* Indeed, *social being ("das gesellschaftliche Sein")* is explained through dialectical materialism as the product of a genesis.

Would it be too much to assume that Lukács consciously or unconsciously seeks the *foundation* of a dialectical materialism in *an ontology?* But in this case, it is not Hartmann whom he should have chosen as a model, but rather the theologians, as did Hegel. Indeed, it is at this point that we find support for our assumption that Lukács found at least the idea of an ontology *in the theologians* when searching for the foundation of ethics.

Although theology is not ontology, it contains certain elements of the latter, e.g., some form of *genesis* and *teleology.* Furthermore, theology is also subject to the law of its own internal consistency.

Now, the notion of *genesis* offers itself as the best illustration of what we mean by the *internal consistency* of doctrines; it exemplifies also why ontology is the best way of testing this *internal consistency.* If Lukács wants to maintain (and eventually he does) that *social being* is the product of a *genesis,* he will be compelled to accept in his ontology notions that otherwise he would have shunned.

He rightly stated at the beginning of his *Ontology of Social Being* that "social being has several domains and all of them seem to be subject to the same kind of necessity and order of laws as nature itself."[24] Hence the idea of a "general ontology" and the assertion that inorganic nature is somehow the foundation of all being, including social being: this is indeed the reformulation of the principle of materialism.

What Lukács has not foreseen, but what he had to realize in the course of the elaboration of his ontology, is that principles once stated command the law of consistency, and they are tested in their implications. *Genesis*—the emergence of beings—implies a whole series of questions (whence, how, why); it will reintroduce the "philosophical half-solutions" that Hartmann eliminated through his conception of ontology as a *descriptive* science of being, and it will be the occasion for numerous pitfalls that Lukács did not foresee. We shall analyze his paper on ontology to show his struggle in the concrete. But we can also sum up our remarks in an *analytic* proposition: who says *genesis,* says also *hypothesis.* With this statement we have forced Lukács into a contradiction with himself. Has he not valued Hartmann especially for his opposition to hypotheses? But again, it was feasible for Hartmann because he stopped at the categories, and in doing so stopped short of *genesis.* Categories, considered alone, can be descriptive, and for this reason they need not be grounded on hypotheses. But in such categories the *content ("Gehalt")* remains necessarily unknown. Consequently, Hartmann will affirm the emergence of something purposive *("Zweckmässige")* out of that which is purposeless *("aus Zwecklosen")*.[25] Such reasoning is perfectly in line with his *descriptive ontology,* or, as Lukács says in conversation with Hans-Dieter Bahr, objective ontology, but, we must note, it is incompatible with the notion of *genesis,* which, according to its nature, requires the knowledge of the *content* of categories and an inherent purposiveness, or teleology.[26] Genesis, then, is unthinkable without *hypotheses* (or presuppositions). This is an example of how Lukács's arguments meet in a pitfall or wheel around under the inexorable law of *internal consistency.*

But then, the law of *internal consistency* is a boomerang in the hands of all those who attempt to found an ontology. In such a way, Lukács can also use it against Hartmann, when, on the one hand, he praises his neutrality, and, on the other hand, he sees in this neutrality a handicap forcing Hartmann into inevitable contradictions (p. 180).

However, Lukács failed to see that Hartmann's neutrality is consistent with his ontological method: description in the phenomenological sense lacks presuppositions. If the all-important notion of *genesis* is lacking in this system, there is a replacement for it, which also escaped Lukács's attention: *time*. But *time* is not equivalent to *history*, which, in the Lukácsian sense, has its laws, but rather is the *horizon* where *change* is observed and *meaning* emerges. But again, the emergence of meaning must be taken in the *descriptive* sense, that is, as an *inventory* of meanings that does not exclude the coexistence of the meaningful and the contradictory. Searching for an ultimate reason would transform the world from an open world (*"die sinnoffene Welt"*) into a world where new meanings could not arise (*"sinngeschlossene Welt")*[27].

This misunderstanding of Hartmann's ontology produced further misinterpretations, because of the law of implications. This is how consistency produces consecutive blunders. The misunderstanding of a notion of time that cannot be considered the equivalent of time in history resulted in Lukács's criticism of Hartmann's neglect of everyday life and work. Once more, Lukács overlooked the implications of Hartmann's descriptive ontology, and on account of this bias he produced his consecutive blunders: he blamed Hartmann for not understanding the role of labor and its starting point (p. 210).

Lukács's Conception of Ontology

What is Lukács's main thesis? "Social being has several domains and all of them seem to be subject to the same kind of necessity and order of laws as nature itself."[28]

In the past, philosophers attempted to solve the question of social being by introducing different kinds of laws, but succeeded only in splitting reality, as Kant did, into two realms that could not be reunited.

As a result, there always arise methodological compromises that set aside the fundamental ontological problem concerning the ontological particularity of social being and approach the difficulties of a specific domain from epistemological or purely methodological and scientific points of view. . . . It was Marx himself who first posited the problem [of *social being*] in its proper perspective. He had a clear understanding that there is a whole range of categorical determinations which are necessary whenever the ontological character of a concrete being is to be grasped. Therefore, the ontology of social being presupposes a general ontology. But this should not be turned again into a theory of knowledge. There is no question of an analogy between a general theory of knowledge and the specific methods of individual sciences. The case is rather that what is known through a general ontology is nothing else than the general ontological foundations of each being. In reality complicated ontological forms take shape (life, society); but the categories of the general ontology must be retained in them as moments of the changes ["*als aufgehobene Momente*"]; the surpassing ["*Aufheben*"] has rightly in Hegel also the significance of conservation ["*Aufbewahren*"].

General ontology, or to say the same in a concrete way, the ontology of inorganic nature as foundation of every being, is general in the sense that there is no being whose ontological foundation does not originate somehow in inorganic nature. New categories may arise in life, but they acquire their ontological efficiencies only on the basis of general categories and in interaction with them. In the same way, new categories of social being adapt themselves to those of organic and inorganic nature. The question concerning the essence and characteristics of social being raised by Marx can only be made intelligible on the ground of such foundation as has degrees, or levels. The question concerning the particularlity of social being implies the affirmation of the unity of each being and at the same time that of the occurrence of its specific determination."[29]

Then Lukács lists, according to the tradition of this science, the ontological presuppositions that are the cornerstones of the system.

The *first* is the basic tenet of materialism: inorganic nature is the foundation of all beings, hence the interconnectedness of all beings, including social being. "New categories may arise in life, but they acquire their ontological efficiencies only on the basis of general categories and in interaction with them."

The internal consistency of the system commands interconnectedness even on the level of social being, on the ground of the first basic categories of inorganic and organic being. That presupposition which insures the unity of the system is *Widerspiegelung* — reflection.

The next presupposition is *praxis*. Lukács considers the introduction of this notion the most decisive change in the traditional way of thinking. Marx states this notion in his famous eleventh thesis on Feuerbach. Lukács affirms that these ontological principles are already exhibited in Marx's work and that these are the ones that unite the otherwise unbridgeable dualism in reality encountered by earlier thinkers from Aristotle to Kant and Hegel.

Then Lukács makes an astonishing statement: "Up to now, there is no history of ontology" (p. 8). He attributes this shortcoming to the lack of clarity and mistakes in pre-Marxist ontology. From his criticism of previous systems we learn more about Lukács's conception of ontology. Ontology should be, if not scientific, based on science, incorporating the discoveries of an age and, at the same time, it should be purely theoretical *("auf das rein Principielle beschränkend")*. The term "scientific" should not make one think only of those elements that pertain to the higher organization of nature; this investigation, which starts out on the lowest level of social being, the level of everyday-ness, is also scientific. Even Nicolai Hartmann, whom Lukács held in high esteem on the ground of his ontological speculations, has overlooked the importance of this seemingly modest phenomenon.

Although Lukács praises Marx for being the first to place the problem of social being in its proper perspective, he acknowledges his indebtedness to Nicolai Hartmann for showing the right direction in the elaboration of an ontology.

What are Hartmann's special merits, as perceived by Lukács?[30]

1. For Hartmann ontology is not the metaphysical end result (*"Endergebnis"*) of philosophy.

2. He has eliminated the thing-in-itself (*"Ding an sich"*) from philosophy, thus presenting total reality.

3. He had no interest in religious problems, either in their classical forms or in their modern appearances.

4. He built ontology from below (*"von unten"*) starting with the primitive form of reality and not with the highest (*"von oben"*).

What is the foundation of ontology in this sense? It is based on *phenomena* — what shows itself, what is visible — and not on *hypotheses*. Furthermore, ontology is not a theory of knowledge. "Erkenntnis gibt es nur von dem, was erst einmal 'ist' " ("There is knowledge only of that which already 'exists' ") (p. 178).

Have we stressed unduly the influence of Hartmann on Lukács and left that of Hegel unnoticed? Indeed, Lukács wrote a historical chapter on Hegel, and entitled it "Hegel's False and True Ontology," implying that in addition to his errors Hegel also had merit. Nevertheless, Hegel's idealism remains for Lukács a theology that explains being *from above ("von oben")*. Therefore, considering the basic conception of ontology, Hartmann takes precedence over Hegel, whose idealism Lukács described as a materialism turned upside down (*"auf dem Kopf gesetzten Materialismus"*).[31]

Is There an Abridged Version of the *Ontology*?

From our presentation it appears that we have in the *Ontology* a major work of Marxist philosophy. Now, we could go on and speculate how far the *Ontology* was completed to Lukács's satisfaction, since his death put an end to all possible revisions. Those, like his disciples Agnes Heller, György Márkus, Mihály Vajda, and Ferenc Fehér, who wished to have the *Ontology* revised may claim that Lukács would have done so, if he had had the time. However, it is easy to maintain also that he would not have changed anything essential in this work. A conversation Lukács had with his disciples not long before his death suggests the latter alternative.[32] We have in addition the support of another evidence, the paper Lukács prepared for the Fourteenth International Congress of Philosophy held in Vienna at the beginning of September 1968. As Lukács says, it contains the essential elements of his major work, the *Ontology of Social Being*. This paper, for reasons not available to us, was never delivered. Everyone recalls that the Congress coincided with the Russian invasion of Prague. Whatever the circumstances that prevented Lukács from delivering this paper, they do not lessen the importance of this little work. It is published in English translation for the first time as Appendix II to this book.

This paper, to which we refer as the "Vienna paper,"[33] bears the following title: "Die ontologischen Grundlagen des menschlichen Denkens und Handelns" ("The Ontological Foundations of Human Thinking and Action"). Due to its comprehensive nature, concise form, and authenticity—Lukács published it himself, first in *Ad lectors 8,* then in a selection of his works in Hungarian[34]—the Vienna paper reveals the virtues and vices of this new ontology better than the complete version. Therefore it becomes a daring adventure compared to the long commentary on Hegel and on Marx. But for reasons unknown to us, this little work has not been included in the complete works of Lukács as published by Luchterhand. It seems, then, appropriate to bring it to the attention of a wider circle of readers.

In the following pages, I shall not only analyze this paper, but later, in discussing the objections of Lukács's disciples to the *Ontology,* I offer readers an opportunity to judge for themselves how far the Vienna paper already contains almost all the elements that surface in the criticism of the "Budapest School," published several years after Lukács's death and based on the complete text of the *Ontology.*

The Vienna Paper

Lukács declares at the outset of his Vienna paper that he will not deal with ontologies of the last decade, because he considers the success of these undertakings doubtful. He cites Sartre as an example. His concern is to show the relationship of these ontologies to Marxism, which until now has not been considered an ontology, although the philosophy which originates in Marx is the theoretical and practical foundation of a historical ontology of materialism (p. 136).

Lukács credits Marx with the launching of a new era, since Marx did away with the "logico-deductive element" and the teleology of the Hegelian philosophy. This "correction" in the spirit of materialism put an end to the synthesis of a primitive beginning as cause of the process. The starting point in Marx is neither the atom of the materialists of antiquity, nor an abstract being, as in Hegel. Every being in Marx has to be an objective being; every being has to be at the same time an active and passive component of a concrete totality. Therefore, Marx's ontology is based on the historical process. Consequently, even the usually stable elements, the categories, undergo change with time. Lukács warns against a too-literal interpretation of Marx, which leads to the subordination of consciousness on the ground that consciousness is a "late product of the ontological evolution of matter." Lukács notes that according to the philosophy of evolution of materialism a late product is not necessarily inferior from an ontological point of view (pp. 136-37).

The exposition of the ontology of social being follows these remarks. It includes the exposition of the complete world order, since social being is dependent on organic being and the latter owes its existence to its inorganic foundation. Hence the importance of the Vienna paper does not consist in its completeness but in its effort to assert the unity and place of all beings, including those most delicate cases for a theory such as Marxism: qualitative differentiation and the exceptions to the rule. The whole theory evolves through the intricate ordering of freedom, necessity, and evolution; matter and consciousness; work and response. In spite of its characteristic vocabulary, which is reminiscent of the Marxist tradition, the Vienna paper is written in the vein of ontologies, and therefore it is appropriate to question the success of Lukács's undertaking, judging it on the basis of this summary of his ontological position.

Comments on the Vienna Paper

First, in retaining his fidelity to Marx, Lukács repudiates metaphysical causality in both of its forms — that linked with a belief in God and that linked with the Hegelian idea of beginning. Lukács even makes a profession of faith by reiterating the fundamental principle of Marx: "the primacy of the material factor with respect to the essence and constitution of social being" (p. 149).[35] But the law of consistency soon compels him to impose a limitation on the first principle of his ontology: "the materialistic conception of reality has nothing in common with the nowadays-so-frequent capitulation before the objective and subjective particularities of beings" (p. 149). It would be of importance for us to know what philosophical doctrine Lukács considered to be a capitulation before subjective and objective particularities. I think it is possible to say, without any injustice to Lukács or others, that he had the positivists in mind.

But it is more important to find out what Lukács wanted to accomplish by trying to retain objective and subjective particularities. Could it be maintained that he tried to broaden Marxism in order to make room for the "qualitative," the "unlawful" phenomena? I think that this thesis could be advanced, based on the chapter on Hegel in the *Ontology of Social being*.[36] Lukács states here that the older form of materialism was unable to incorporate into its system the qualitative. He attributes this shortcoming to the far too rigid form of materialism that prevailed during the Enlightenment. Thus, as we see, Lukács alluded to Diderot, rather than to Marx; whether this was to avoid conflict with Marxism remains a hypothesis.

Nevertheless, Lukács broaches this question by referring to some "useless" innovations, which are engraved in the memory of people and which survive much longer than the ones that have transformed the economic life of mankind. He mentions the exceptional men who were able to make a step towards the better realization of man in man. What does he really mean? The only concrete examples he gives are the admiration of Lenin for the Appassionata of Beethoven (p. 148) and the influence of great men on Marx. However, he does not go very far in this direction, because he elsewhere calls Heidegger a bourgeois romantic philosopher.[37] Are we to conclude that a bourgeois cannot be a great man or a romantic a great poet? Perhaps even his opponents would agree that Heidegger has, after all, "some" talent. Would the law of exceptions allow the mystics and perhaps even the saints to express a new characteristic of being, a new ontological truth?

Although Lukács does not follow out his own "principle," his statement on objective and subjective particularities is a breakthrough in the philosophy of materialism. The most important implication of this principle (if it can be called a principle, and not just a statement) is that by this Lukács rejects the dialectic of nature in favor of the dialectic of history.[38] This allows us to ask several important questions. Does Lukács proclaim the qualitative differentiation of matter, which is ontological nonsense, or does he allude to something other than the material? Whichever be the case his position already undermines the primacy of the "material" as the first principle of being. This attempt to save what is individual, what is unique, is in conflict with Marx's own position also: human sensibility must become theoretical[39] in the struggle for freedom; this is indeed the "summit of the struggle" (quoted by Lukács himself). Therefore, Lukács's attempt to save the "exceptional" and the "exception," i.e., great men and their "achievements," fails if he keeps the material as his unifying ontological principle.

On the other hand, if Lukács accepts "exception" as another presupposition of his ontology, he opens the door to an infinite series of possibilities for beings; and in this way, he eliminates ontology as a foundation of value judgement. Yet for Lukács, ontology is meant to serve this purpose, for he wanted to use it in the elaboration of his ethics.

The second ontological principle, the first in order of importance, is evolution (p. 137). Evolution is a mysterious *deux ex machina* that governs "becoming." It transforms part of inorganic matter into living organism by the unexplainable "leap" that occurs somewhere in the course of evolution. Lukács holds evolution responsible for the existence of consciousness. Then consciousness sets into motion dialectics by placing itself between freedom and necessity. Consciousness becomes in this way the third ontological principle.[40] Furthermore, consciousness distinguishes man from stone and animals and moves him towards the satisfaction of his first necessities. This it accomplishes by producing a response to what surrounds man and this response we call "work."[41] All this is bundled with necessity, which constrains matter and consciousness to follow a path (pp. 143-46). And if someone asks "which path?" the answer is: the path of evolution.

Thus evolution, the most important ontological principle (besides work), turns out to be an empty concept. It is not logos, it is not reason, it cannot be the irrational, because that would put an end to science (and to Lukács's own title: Marxist scientist). If it is energy, what is its source and whence comes the form that will subdue that unharnessed force? It remains also unanswered whence this occult energy would receive its direction.

As if Lukács wanted to fill this lacuna, he adds at this point another principle, teleology, teleology humanized, which means that man transforms his world and transforms himself (p. 143). This transformation is carried out as a response or human reaction by means of work, the most important ontological principle besides evolution. Labor and evolution constitute the two principal poles of this ontology. Evolution is the occult force of nature, a kind of necessity that man cannot control, and work affirms the presence and determination of man to shape his world. Since work has an aim, a direction given by consciousness, teleology will find its place between work and consciousness. This way of conceiving teleology is a reformulation of the old concept, whose efficiency depended on a higher principle and was therefore responsible for the organization and "evolution" of beings in the universe. In Lukács's ontology, teleology is limited to the "local" and utilitarian organization of man's surroundings and receives its direction through work from man, the only conscious agent in Lukács's universe. Lukács says that thanks to this new conception of teleology we do not need to invent a transcendental subject or a special efficiency in order to attribute teleological tendencies to nature and to society (p. 139).

Nevertheless, Lukács did not succeed in reshaping ontology completely. Although he harnessed teleology by putting it under the command of consciousness and making it subservient to labor, which suggests complete control of man over his potentialities, causality, the mainspring of classical ontology, finds its way back into this new system. "Labor," says Lukács, "is composed of teleological positionings that activate causal series" (p. 139). It would be interesting to know to what extent man is in control of these causal series. Because, if man triggers, but does not control, this new efficiency, it becomes doubtful whether we are the "makers of our world" in the sense Lukács would like; perhaps we should say that another efficiency, a hidden teleology or a logos, which escapes our vigilance, is setting the pace of change and evolution. If the latter is the case, and it is difficult to understand Lukács's statement otherwise, his ontology becomes a desperate struggle against the same inscrutable powers that classical metaphysics labelled in different ways.[42]

Main Features of the Vienna Paper's Ontology

If we sum up the main features of Lukács's ontology as expressed in the Vienna paper, we may say that by rejecting the dialectic of nature in favor of the dialectic of history Lukács rejects "the domination of spontaneous and mechanic necessity" and replaces it by a necessity originating in a teleological genesis, which has important consequences in all social processes.[43] His ontology is situated, in this way, at the level of social activity. However, he keeps the old characteristics of necessity: stimulation, constraint, and pressure. A revised form of evolutionism constitutes the foundation of social activity in the following sense: the different degrees of perfection in beings are the product or result of successive stages of development, but at the same time, each level is separated from the preceding one by a leap.[44]

At the beginning, I called ontology a test of consistency; therefore, I may now raise the questions which are the consequences of Lukács's ontological positions and ask how they affect Marxism in general.

The most difficult question for every ontology is to explain the dualism of material and spiritual, or body and mind. Lukács's material principle is supposed to produce its counterpart—consciousness, i.e., intelligence; or, in other terms, if Lukács is right in saying that quantitative change can produce qualitative results, he has to readmit Engels's dialectic of nature, which he wanted to reject in order to make room for the dialectic of history. Lukács also has to reject the revised form of teleology that he places between work and consciousness, because the dialectic of nature subsumes teleology under itself.

On the other hand, if his principle of evolution admits leaps that are responsible for the production of higher categories of being, Lukács destroys the dialectic of nature with its necessity, which serves as a teleology in this system. Also, at the same time, he destroys his own theory of evolution. Indeed, the leap reveals a rupture in the dialectical system; it indicates the breakdown of mediation (*Aufhebung*) and in this way introduces the unexpected, the unforeseeable. On the other hand, if leaps were part of the ontological order, this would mean the compartmentation of evolution and the positing of fixed entities that would serve as limits to evolution. Then, these fixed entities would hinder and divert the movement of dialectics, which is the explanatory factor in Lukács's ontology. As a consequence, these entities or species would remain unexplained, or their explanation would necessitate the introduction of some form of creationism or fixism, i.e., the preexistence of forms or ideas, because these species would not be the products, but the starting points of a limited dialectical activity. Furthermore, in order to be starting points, they should bear in themselves the dualism or contradiction necessary for their own destruction. Whichever be the case, the insufficiency of the material principle comes to light in the examination of Lukács's ontological presuppositions. As it is, his ontology comes close to Bergson's *évolution créatrice*. Furthermore, if we consent to speak, as Lukács does, of social process, stages of evolution, the possibility or necessity of evolution, we cannot refuse to answer the question of how, by what means, according to what laws, Lukács conceives this process. If everything is due to a leap, namely to chance, is it not chance itself that becomes necessity, the necessity of the unforeseeable?

If it is objected that Lukács refers to the interplay of freedom and necessity in the teleological thematization and to human consciousness as the regulative principle of change and efficiency, we must reply that in Lukács's ontology both freedom and necessity are empty concepts. Necessity is bound to specifications, otherwise it becomes an occult power. In the same way, freedom without purposiveness, ideal, or aim, that is, freedom without real choice, is only chance.

Sometimes the reader is under the impression that Lukács realized the lack of unity of his system, because he tried to introduce something that could correct this shortcoming. When discussing his central ontological principle, labor, he finds it difficult to reconcile labor, teleology, and consciousness with the ontological priority of matter. Then he says that, from an ontological point of view, the "answer," i.e., man's responses to nature through work, precedes the question. How is one to interpret this thesis? Does Lukács resort to a subterfuge to introduce some intelligence into material necessity? This intelligence would then emerge as the point of contact with the problem. But in this case, we should suppose a question inherent in matter, primary source of all change and becoming (p. 138). Is it not, in a way, suggesting the intelligence of matter? Or, if this is unacceptable to Lukács because it suggests the dualism of body and soul, would it not be necessary to admit a force that comes second to intelligence, namely, desire or instinct? Let us assume that this would explain at least the beginning of the process. But in that case the response would be prior to the emergence of consciousness, and that would be teleology inherent in desire, the desire of matter, hence of some intelligence.

Lukács labors hard to provide a consistent answer to the question of being without the help of the traditional resources of ontologies. So far, as we have seen, he has not been very successful. His ontology is lacking the original thrust that would provide both unity and movement for his explanation. The material principle as well as the revised form of evolution and his modified teleology fail to work satisfactorily. As it is presented in his Vienna paper, Lukács's ontology is a "chassé-croisé"[45] of principles, which, as I have pointed out, may lead even to a transcendental subject, or a spirit (*Geist*), or a *logos,* in spite of the author's vehement protest against all of them. We may conclude that all the way through we have the impression that Lukács's ontology is in quest of its own origin.

The difficulties I have listed may account for Lukács's flight from the realm of ontology proper to his favorite field — class struggle — and what is associated with it, economism and a kind of social analysis.[46] In this field, we have to grant, Lukács presents subtle analyses of particular phenomena, but this is not exactly the way to argue out ontological principles. Although Lukács gives a plausible explanation of the appearance of a new reality, he does not follow up the consequences of his partial findings. Thus, applied to being in general, this explanation often yields an unacceptable conclusion, or his ontological concepts become empty due to contradictory or inadequate assertions (as we have seen above in the case of evolution and freedom). In other terms, getting lost in the analysis of social phenomena, Lukács does not realize that he elevates "operational concepts" to the rank of ontological principles. For example, taking work as an explanatory factor, Lukács is able to elucidate a great number of phenomena, but could it be maintained that the response man gives in his work explains also all cultural and religious[47] manifestations of human existence? The essential of what we call culture or a way of life is perhaps more than simply a way to survive.

I have affirmed that ontology as a pure theory becomes its own measure; it also becomes, then, the measure of Lukács's achievement in this field. Indeed, it reveals the inconsistencies, the leaps, and the lacunae in his philosophy. For this reason his ontology leaves the impression that it tends to justify and sometimes perhaps amend a political theory. Therefore, I consider that there is sufficient ground to call his ontology an appendix to praxis, namely, an ideology.

Controversy Around the *Ontology*

This judgment seems to contradict our appreciation of Lukács's *Ontology* as a theoretical work comparable to other ontologies that were *not* associated with a political order.

In our defense, we could still say that it was possible to present this view on the ground of the inconsistencies found in Lukács's paper, and we did it by questioning the implications of Lukács's presuppositions. This is the only way—all metaphysicians know it, and A.N. Whitehead also taught us—to test the applicability of the system.

Let us now assume that Lukács wanted it the way he did, or at least that for the time being he wished not to pursue the reform of Marxism any further. His dilemma will always be the same: for some, he did not go far enough, for others he was too innovative.

I accept the responsibility for saying that Lukács did not go far enough, and I lay this accusation in the name of philosophy (or ontology) proper, which is the interpretation of the world by means of speculations. Interpretation, on the other hand, is a sort of answering of the questions one raises when confronted with extra-mental reality and with the reality of consciousness. The critique of a philosophy consists then in the examination of the scope of the answers. In sum, it is possible to list the *unanswered* questions, which I have done, on the basis of Lukács's attempts *to give answers* to problems encountered in *praxis*. It is also possible to criticize the answer itself and to propose different versions when interpreting reality. This latter could already be qualified as biased criticism, because it would impose on Lukács presuppositions other than his own; for example, the dualism of *matter* and *spirit* instead of his *materialist principle*. Being well aware of the risks of my undertakings—and by this I mean, first of all, the risk of being accused of rejecting Lukács's interpretation of reality—I have consciously avoided this path. Hence, qualifying Lukács's interpretation of reality in the Vienna paper as a form of ideology, in spite of its innovations, because it tries to justify a *praxis,* is completely in line with the fundamental principles of an ontology to be the science of being as being. Indeed, who could find, even among the *orthodox* Marxist colleagues, someone who would associate Aristotle's *Metaphysics* (ontology) with the contemporary economic or social structure, and affirm that his presuppositions would be the *reflections* of a social and economic order built on slavery? Whatever be the evaluation of Aristotle's other works, his *Metaphysics* and *Physics,* which is also a metaphysics, stand out as exceptions. The same question could be asked about Hartmann's *Ontology,* which appeared to be a model for Lukács.

What a paradox, then, to see Lukács's own disciples, who are sometimes called "l'école de Budapest," confirm our own findings, based on what could be called a summary of the *Ontology;* namely, that in the completed work Lukács was trying to work out a compromise between ontology and ideology! More precisely, Lukács attempted to give a theoretical foundation to *Marxist parxis* and not simply to *human thinking and action,* as its title suggests. If, in my opinion, Lukács has not gone far enough, l'école de Budapest is convinced that he went too far, or more exactly, that he went astray. In a sort of solemn proclamation, they enumerate their master's deviations from the right path, and they lay this accusation in the name of Lukács's earlier position (that is, prior to the *Ontology*) and on the basis of what has been accepted so far as *orthodox,* that is, faithful to Marx. By so doing, Lukács's disciples judge their master in the name of Marxist ideology and indicate clearly that this is what they expected him to write. In this way, they confirm what seemed to be a too-severe criticism, that Lukács remained on the threshold of ontology, or half-way beween ideology and ontology. But this "half-way" was already too much for his disciples, who wanted to appear more orthodox or more authentic than their master.

It is obvious that we would not want to reopen the question of orthodoxy (or authenticity) since we have found it fruitless to discuss such notions and because we have replaced it by what seemed to us a safer standard — the internal consistency of a life and doctrine.

Nevertheless, one cannot help wondering why these Marxist philosophers decided to come before public opinion and inculpate their master, especially so many years after Lukács's death. Their critique was published in English in *Telos,* and in Italian in another Marxist periodical, *Aut-Aut.*[48] It reads as follows:

> First, the *Ontology* — Lukács's last ambitious work, written while his health was still intact — is now being published in Hungarian, in German, and now also in Italian . . . There is the brute fact that he did not regard the manuscript he left us as the final version . . . Secondly, after Lukács's death — partly but not primarily in connection with the publication of his Ontology — we were often asked to clarify our own relation to his last creative period, especially since disagreements about the Ontology had also appeared in print (in *Der Spiegel,* June 14, 1971).

In view of the increasingly sharper theoretical debates and the ever more personal atmosphere towards the end of his life, overcast by the painful shadow of extreme old age, another question is justified: Why didn't we bring our differences of opinion before the public? Aside from circumstances we do not wish to elaborate on now and which could be considered secondary factors in our decision, we agreed not to formulate *during his lifetime* as a public polemic against him the things we had repeatedly said to him in private. He was informed of our decision and agreed fully with it . . . About our own motives, with which Lukács was in full accord, we can only say that it was and remains our conviction that there can and ought to be intellectual differences—even essential ones—between philosophers who are in fundamental agreement.

Another sentence sums up the reason for writing and publishing these "Notes" on the *Ontology:* "the 'Notes' incontestably signal a parting of philosophical ways . . ." (pp. 162–69).

The reasons given for the publication of the "Notes," however, do not explain the delay: Lukács died in June 1971, the article in *Telos* came out in the fall of 1976; its preface is dated January 1975.

In the meantime the four—Ferenc Fehér, Agnes Heller, György Márkus, and Mihály Vajda—lost their positions in the Hungarian Academy of Science. This information is printed at the end of the special issue on Lukács in *Aut-Aut.*[49] Then, one may raise the question whether their action was not politically motivated.[50] The remarks—"the 'Notes' incontestably signal a parting of philosophical ways . . ." point in this direction. But I would not speculate any further, since my concern is the *content* of the writers' accusations rather than their motives. This is, indeed, the only profitable undertaking, since trying to settle a dispute when families are in an open feud (and one could qualify the intervention of Lukács's disciples as such a feud) is a waste of energy. Family feuds are not uncommon in "ideological households." A quarrel of this kind is usually a fight over terminology, as we witness when reading the accusations against *History and Class Consciousness.* We find examples of it in Novack: Lukács rejected the dialectic of nature and applied dialectic only to the social, the historical; idealistic deviation is a similar accusation. The general characteristic of a "family feud" is that it is fought not on the ground of *principles,* but by means of *words.* The accusations of Lukács's disciples are of such nature; they also clearly indicate that their authors have not understood what ontology is as a science of being in general. Therefore, the reader of their article can be easily misled by their seeming agreement with Lukács so far as the general intent of their master went. "In discussing our relation to the Ontology retrospectively more than a decade after the beginning of the work, we should mention the incredibly intense liberating effect that this intellectual enterprise and the setting of its objective had on all of us," they write. Then, they add what constitutes for me as well the essence of this unusual venture in Marxism: "Since our philosophical childhood, we had sought a *'philosophy of practice'* "; (p. 163 *italics mine*). This means that they have realized themselves that *extending* Marxism was an impasse, but that "reviewing the whole" far exceeded their strength. It is understandable why Lukács's decision to write *The Ontology of Social Reality* had such a "liberating effect on [them]," because it was also a guarantee of success. In sum, Lukács's disciples discovered either on their own, or in conversation with their master, that "traditional Marxism" needed revision and continuation in order to be able to face the challenge of modern times: "We expected," they write, "a work that would carry out a synthesis between historicism and analysis on the universal generic level, between practice-centeredness and philosophical universality." And they conclude: "Thus we formulated our expectations of the Ontology rather sketchily, but also more concretely than a mere longing for a 'great work' " (p. 164).

Whether the formulation of the task to be accomplished is theirs or their teacher's, it correctly expresses "the century-old dilemma of Marxism as philsosophy" (p. 166).

My suspicion, however, is that the disciples only echoed their teacher's preoccupation, which is, after all, not to their discredit. Did they not live with him, as they say, almost in daily contact and discussion during the last part of the 1950s and during the 1960s, when Lukács worked on his *Ontology?* My suspicion is, then, further confirmed by their inability to understand what ontology is, since they blamed their teacher for abandoning former solutions or deviating from the Marxist line. Those who know what ontology is know also that we do not impose our solutions, but rather the opposite is the case: ontology compels us to accept solutions in line with the presuppositions we have chosen at the start. Once Lukács laid down his ontological principles, he was no longer master of the game. The internal logic of ontology drove him ahead and solutions emerged from the context set by the principles that he had chosen. The inconsistencies pointed out by Lukács's disciples may originate, then, either from Lukács's forgetfulness of his chosen principles and their implications, or his reluctance to submit himself, to the very end, to the internal logic of his "new" system.

Another reason to suspect that "the Four" could not cope with the problem, although they have correctly circumscribed it, is that they omit in their background Lukács's own struggle with "the synthesis of practice-centeredness and philosophical universality." They make no allusion to the sources from which Lukács could have taken his examples, but they make mention of Lukács's aversion to the term"ontology," since towards the end of the 1950s he used this expression as an invective rather than as a model for constructive thinking. They also relate Habermas's rejection of the plan of the *Ontology* when it had been presented to him by Agnes Heller in 1966. There is a third reason which I add with certain reservations, but I do so because circumstances indicate its possibility. In conversation with someone who was also close to Lukács, I learned that Lukács wrote the "prolegomena" (which is an introduction) after he completed his work in order to explain to his disciples why he had written the *Ontology*.[51] Although I present this as a hypothesis, we find a quasiconfirmation of this anecdote in the article of the Four, as they relate how they struggled with their teacher to convince him to change his text. They pursued him almost to his death-bed, offering him their help to carry out the correction. They even quote him as saying, when someone wanted to unburden him of some of the technical tasks connected with his work: "I have to clean my own dirty laundry" (p. 162). But he was no longer able to do this.

Since the harassment went on for years, we have reason to think that he did not want to comply with the wishes of his students; instead, he spent the last part of his life writing the prolegomena, hoping to convince them that he was on the right track to solve the problem of the "philosophy of practice." Having failed to see the implications of an ontology serving as the theoretical foundation of praxis—in our terms, the continuation of Marx and the foundation of a Marxist ontology according to Lukács—the critique of the disciples could not aim at the essential, and therefore was unable to offer a valid criticism of the *Ontology*. By valid criticism, we mean again, the examination of the internal consistency of Lukács's doctrine of social being. Their critique remains a criticism from an ideological bias, similar to the kind exercised by mediocre Christians on the doctrine of atheists. In sum, criticisms of this sort are always the application of criteria alien to the intent of the author. It is obvious that not choosing the same presuppositions as a point of departure, they must arrive at different conclusions.

Since the reason an ontology needed to be construed (in order to build upon it an ethics) is not understood by the disciples, their critique is limited only to the details of the execution, and here only to the verification of terminology used by Lukács. It is not only surprising but shocking that they were not interested in the reasons for the changes introduced by Lukács and that they have not presented a more systematic criticism of the *Ontology*.

In this case, what importance, if any, should we attribute to their writings? In sum, a list of crimes, or ideological deviations, resembles more the practice of witchcraft or witch-hunters than a proper court of justice, where arguments are presented to prove or to disprove the accused's innocence. No such arguments are found in the writings of the Four, but we can read there again what is characteristic of ideological family feuds—the disciples' insistence on making the suggested corrections. But Lukács's refusal is the guarantee that we have an *Ontology* which can be called Lukács's own with its merits and faults. I do not want to attribute much importance to insinuations that the *Ontology* has been tampered with.[52] In order to change anything in such a work, one has to be familiar with the subject and, as we have seen, even Lukács's own disciples failed to understand their teacher.

Now that we have ventured again to speak of "values," we propose that the *Ontology* was Lukács's ultimate effort to deliver to posterity not necessarily the revised version of his conviction, but a rationalization of his "political faith." Thus the collating of objections without a unifying principle is not appropriate to this work, which is, by definition, a theoretical work.

Nevertheless, in a paradoxical way, those unorganized, scattered "Notes" of the Four, belonging to the "Budapest school," make visible Lukács's merits as a theoretician of praxis and as a philosopher, who tries to break loose from praxis bound to an ideology.

Furthermore, Agnes Heller and her companions help us to accomplish what would otherwise be — due to the length and nature of the *Ontology* — an impossible task. They draw the attention of intellectuals interested in Marxism to the highlights of the *Ontology* and sum up systematically the most important innovations of Lukács. Indeed, they list all those elements in the *Ontology* that either contradict Lukács's earlier position or that of the orthodox line in Marxism. Out of their "Notes" we shall choose only those objections that help us to reconstrue the fabric of the *Ontology*. This is to conform to the ground rules of ontology in general, a science that is renowned for its austerity. Hopefully, in this way we shall be able to unveil another paradox: nowadays, even non-Marxist intellectuals shrink away from the difficult task of working out a synthesis of facts and laws — what we called earlier "metaphysics"; therefore, Lukács's philosophical merit, of having understood the necessity of such a venture, has gone unnoticed even by those who had earlier hailed his ideological revisionism.

Commentary on the "Notes"

Whoever undertakes the task of commenting on the objections assembled by Lukács's disciples faces two difficulties: first, they indicated in note 7 of their article in *Telos* that "pages are given for the original typed manuscript." It would be, then, easy for anyone consulting this manuscript to verify the text and the context before considering the objections. However, the manuscript available in the Lukács Archives in Budapest has a different pagination.[53] Second, the "Notes" are only scattered objections, having no unifying principle that would make this evaluation easier. After all, to oppose a solution given by Lukács in the *Ontology* is one thing; to give a reason for it quite another.

If our principle of the internal consistency of a doctrine as the criterion of success in ontological speculations holds true, one deviation from the right way should necessarily lead to other deviations. That is to say, Lukács or his student could systematically err; these systematic "mistakes" constitute the novelty of the *Ontology* of Lukács and also of the criticism of his disciples.

Therefore, it must be possible to free from the context of the "Notes" a leitmotiv that will make explicit the underlying principle upon which the essential disagreement with Lukács stands, or which explains the disciples' systematic misunderstanding of their master. As a starting point for our elaboration, we will examine whether Lukács's students understood the main thrust of the *Ontology*. The old saying still holds true: "Quia parvus error in principio magnus est in fine . . ." ("Because a little error at the beginning becomes great at the end . . .").

First of all, were they able to measure the immensity of the task when they expected the *Ontology* to be *nothing more than a synthesis,* i.e., "the transcending of purely historicizing tendencies without becoming entangled in the net of 'universal laws' "? (p. 165). They, encouraged by Lukács's enterprise, "seek to work out the central problems of Marxist philosophy—but without, of course, claiming the systematic universality of Lukács's book" (p. 165). Is it not a contradiction in itself to seek to work out the *central problem* without arriving at systematic universality? What provides universality if not that which is central, or fundamental? Hence, all the achievements they list (in note 4, p. 165)—*Marxism and Anthropology,* by György Márkus, or *Objective View of Nature and Social Practice,* by Mihály Vajda, to mention only two—cannot claim to have achieved their goal because there cannot be several central issues, or several *first principles.* They can only rehearse, with slight changes, the old material of a Marxism that so far has never tried to achieve "systematic unviersality." For this reason, even Lukács's failure becomes a great "moral victory" in the sense that it is a giant step towards *intellectual honesty.* Ontology, as we have defined it, is the test of internal consistency which is the highest form of autocriticism.

But Lukács's students are right in saying that the outline of "the most essential problems" can only be replaced "by extensive studies or multi-volume monographs" (p. 167). Indirectly this confirms our assertion that it is possible to list the ontological principles that form the underlying structure of a philosophy without entering into discussion of the author's application of these principles to special issues. Therefore, we shall use these notes exactly with this intention: to offer a starting point for further analyses of the *Ontology.* However, this aim will be achieved only if we are able to show the "systematic universality" of the work under discussion. This "systematic universality" then supercedes "local" contradictions, concessions to ideology and praxis, and a fidelity to Marx that Lukács wants to retain even at the risk of inconsistencies.

On the whole, the following rule holds: inconsistencies in the details, that is, in the application of principles, can be attributed to faulty reasoning, which results from improper drawing of implications; changes of principles, on the contrary, are forced upon a philosophy by the internal logic of its presuppositions; as an example, we note the broadening of *vulgar* materialism into a *dialectical* materialism, since the latter is able to explain those phenomena that are out of the reach of the former. As we have seen earlier, Lukács's purpose was the *broadening* and *continuation* of Marxism; hence any change of principles in the *Ontology* must be viewed as imposed on Lukács by circumstances, i.e., by phenomena that are left unexplained even by dialectical materialism. We may list Engel's *Dialectic of Nature* as a work which sought early the "systematic universality" mentioned by the Budapest school. However, that attempt has been deemed a failure by Lukács in his *History and Class Consciousness;* hence, the reformulation of principles to insure the desired "systematic universality" became necessary.

The first question to be answered here is: what kind of science or philosophical discipline, what method, is suitable to realize the synthesis of existing methods into a universal synthesis of all phenomena, into a "systematic universality"? What should be the starting point? We have seen Lukács's answer. Now, what improvement do the four members of the Budapest school suggest if they are disappointed with Lukács's solution? If the solution does not satisfy them, they must also be disappointed with his first principle. The "Notes" leave the question unanswered. On our part, we have affirmed that the disciples could not follow Lukács in his search for an answer to the question, which means that they do not understand what ontology is. The accusation is very serious, because if it is substantiated, it can invalidate the criticism found in the "Notes." How shall we support our contention, then?

The "Notes" object to Lukács that he has not chosen the proper starting point: "the basic question is not whether philosophy occupies itself with epistemology or with ontology but whether its point of departure is the isolated (necessarily exclusively knowing) individual, or social totality" (p. 171, note 4).

Lukács has formulated the task of ontology at the beginning of the manuscript, in a chapter entitled *"Die gegenwärtige Problemlage — Einführung":* "The ontology of social being has several domains which seem to be clearly subject to necessity and to laws of nature itself" (p. 2). The consequences of this position are that these laws cannot be imposed on social being in the manner of an epistemology, as is the case in the Kantian doctrine, which separates what can be known from what cannot be known. Positivism follows essentially the same trend. Therefore, speaking of Hartmann's ontology,

Lukács states the problem in those terms: "One of the most important methodological problems of ontology is to keep its categories away from all determinations that originate in efforts to dominate the world through thinking" (p. 191).

Lukács is right in insisting on the separation of ontology from epistemology, especially when he has in mind the dominating epistemological trends of the nineteenth century. Neo-Kantianism and neopositivism exemplify a kind of subjectivism which does not recognize the independent existence of reality, hence they go against Lukács's basic ontological principle — *matter,* which leads Lukács towards a kind of realism that we can formulate with Hartmann: "Erkenntnis gibt es nur von dem, was erstmal 'ist'." (p. 178). This statement also indicates the order of priorities: there is only knowledge of that which already exists. Ontology precedes epistemology; furthermore, "general ontology is the condition *sine qua non* of an ontology of social being" (p. 3). This is the reason why the starting point is shifted away from the "individual, or social totality," so that a synthesis of reality — organic, inorganic, and social — could be contrived from below (*"von unten"*). Social being, the disciples should admit, is a later product and dependent on *consciousness.*

Again, it is ontology not epistemology, that explains the distinction between different kinds of beings. Thus ontology also explains the division of beings according to their ontological order. If the first principle is the material, it is evident that "the economic sphere (will be) the essence of the process of reproduction, but everything else belongs to the phenomenal sphere. Consequently, capitalism and socialism differ only in the phenomenal sphere . . " (note 1, p. 171). The disciples object to Lukács that this statement "most drastically contradicts the paper on democratization" (p. 171).

The paper on democratization was not made available to me, and therefore I cannot comment on it; but I would not want to mix issues, either. The *Ontology* speaks for itself: the material principle implies necessity; hence the economic sphere, as the *essence* of the processes of reproduction, is "also the terrain of necessity." If capitalism and socialism differ only in the phenomenal sphere, this means that on the level of reproduction they both face the same laws of *economy,* but they may respond in a different way to problems arising out of such contexts.[54] The *essential* and *phenomenal* spheres *are degrees of being* properly identifiable in an ontological system. If we pursue further the implications of the material principle, we necessarily come to the phenomenal sphere when confronted with the problem of *consciousness.*

The authors of the "Notes" remind us that "in the chapter on *Labor* consciousness becomes a specific form of *non-being* (p. 481) and non-reality" (cf.

note 2). Then, Lukács was consistent at least in his use of the term *phenomenal:* it meant *nonreality* or *non-being;* whereas such being was attributed to both consciousness and the product of consciousness. He followed equally the internal logic of his system when he considered, in the Vienna paper, consciousness as epiphenomenon. The disciples rightly call this the first conception of the *Ontology.* This is followed by the second conception of the *Ontology,* in which "human consciousness does not have epiphenomenal character,"[55] and Lukács's critics point out the inconsistency in the treatment of consciousness. Of course, they are again right; but they should have realized that, this time, inconsistency was forced upon Lukács by the internal logic of reality or *degrees* of *reality* (essential and phenomenal sphere, sphere of *necessity* and sphere of *freedom*). If we conceive man as a responding being (cf. Vienna paper) whence comes the response? If it originates in matter, it will be under the law of *necessity* and consequently all responses will be determined, i.e., all responses will be the same. Reality shows that we have choices and that our responses depend, at least to some extent, on ourselves alone. Therefore, freedom, if it is not a pure illusion — and it would be difficult to maintain that it is only that — demands that our conscousness should not be an epiphenomenon, even if Lukács makes no attempt to say what it is.

The fact remains that when Lukács calls labor the earliest form (*Urform*) of praxis, he resorts to a proof that is under our eyes:

> the bare fact, that realizations (accomplishments of human practice in labor) which came as additions to enter the reality of the world as new kinds of objects (*Gegenständlichkeitsformen*) though not explained through nature, are realities in the same way as the product of nature, proves already at this early stage of our argumenation the validity of our assertion. Of the concrete appearances and exteriorization of consciousness in the same way as of concrete forms of being which do not belong to epiphenomenal characteristics, we shall speak more in this and in the next chapter.[56]

Is it not visible in this "declaration," as Lukács modestly calls it (since he is well aware of the fact that it is not yet a proof), that under the compulsion of reality he is about to broaden Marxism, which forces him into contradiction with his earlier position. His students noticed the contradiction, but failed to understand the reason behind it, since they were guided by their ideology rather than by purely philosophical considerations. Although they mention (p. 166) "the century-old dilemna of Marxism as philosophy: how historicity (history as the only science, to cite Marx) can be reconciled with "systematic

universality"—they do not seem to understand that the internal logic of ontology compels Lukács into concessions, the new conception of consciousness
as *not* an epiphenomenon being one of those concessions. How Lukács was
driven to the recognition of this "new" truth about consciousness appears
clearly from the following text: "It is first in labor, when positing an aim and
its means that consciousness moves with an autonomous act, with a
teleological projection, not only to conform to the environment, an activity
that is proper to animals also that change nature directly, i.e. unconsciously
(*unbeabsichtigt*), but also to carry out changes which are unthinkable, impossible to understand through nature alone." Then Lukács draws the
conclusion from this explanation: "Consciousness can no longer be conceived
ontologically as an epiphenomenon when through its act it becomes a
transforming and innovating principle of nature. With this statement dialectic
materialism distinguishes itself from mechanical materialism which recognizes
only nature as objective reality since it is ordered according to laws."[57]

Of course, Lukács credits Marx with this broadening of Marxism (or
materialism) by quoting: "The fight over the reality or non-reality of thinking—which is isolated from praxis—is only a purely scholastic question."[58]
These interjections, quite frequent, make the reading and evaluation of the
Ontology as an independent and innovative work rather difficult, and the
commentary on this work even hazardous, in the eyes of those who are not accustomed to ontological questions. The above example is an excellent illustration of this state of affairs, for the following reason: it is one thing to state, as
Marx did, that the existence or nonexistence (which is equivalent to the reality
or nonreality) of thought is a scholastic, i.e., an idle question, when it is put independently of praxis; and another to affirm *the independence of consciousness from matter*—for this is what is intended when it is called
"nonepiphenomenal."

Let us test the implications of a consciousness which is an
epiphenomenon, that is, which emerges from matter and hence is bound to
matter somehow or other. Lenin expresses this in the following terms: "Matter
is primary. Sensation, thought, consciousness is the highest product of matter
organized in a certain way. This is the main teaching of materialism and the
teaching of Marx and Engels in particular."[59]

Is the theory of *Widerspiegelung* not based on consciousness being an
epiphenomenon? "Consciousness is an ideal [*ideelle*] *Widerspiegelung* of the
material world, for this reason it has no proper content"—we read further, as a
direct consequence of Lenin's thesis. How can freedom of imagination, inventiveness, be attributed to such a consciousness? How can it create a new reality
(*Wirklichkeit*) not explainable through nature if "it is determined by the
material world"?[60]

Lukács seems to uphold some such thesis that attributes power to consciousness on the ground of observation alone, and he is conscious of it; this is why he speaks of a "declaration," which is to be proved only as the argument progresses. But did Lukács foresee the ontological consequences of his assertion?

If the thesis is proven, the ontological first principle of materialism — *matter* — must be abandoned under the threat of inconsistency. Of course, one may continue to profess political or economic views similar to those held by Marx, but one has to abandon any attempt to speak about aesthetics, ethics, and especially about values related to the phenomenal world of consciousness, because the standard necessary for measuring those realizations will be missing. Among aesthetic realizations we may list a large portion of our everyday life, what is necessary and unnecessary for being and remaining a human being, because the definition of consciousness replaces in materialism (and also in other contemporary philosophical doctrines, e.g., structuralism) the definition of man. Under values we should number all our strivings, including the individual and social, hence the purpose of our activity, education in its broad sense — for life — and in its restricted sense — for a profession. Here we must also list our ways of enjoying ourselves — games and entertainment — our beliefs (cultural and religious), and convictions (ideologies), social, political, artistic, etc.

Ontology, we have said, is a systematic science, which does not tolerate "leaps" in the argument. This is why Lukács had to grant freedom to consciousness by taking it out of the epiphenomenal sphere. But by doing so, he seriously impaired the unity of his system, based as it was on the material principle that implied *Widerspiegelung*. No wonder, therefore, that his disciples take exception to his treatment of the role of consciousness, first, objecting to "the lack of a separate discussion of social objectifications," which, in our mind, means a return to consciousness as epiphenomenon (that is, placing consciousness under the law of necessity); second, objecting that "*the role of consciousness remains unclarified.*"[61] It may be so, but Lukács is quite consistent in his mistake, if it is a mistake, of attempting to raise consciousness above the sphere of necessity.

The disciples list, indeed, as their most important objection to comrade Lukács that he contrasted "objective evolution with its merely subjective reflection (consciousness)," which flows, as we judge it, from the change in the conception of consciousness from an epiphenomenal to nonepiphenomenal nature. Then, they see it as a contradiction to charge consciousness with being "*the bearer of the continuity of social being*" when "the process' objective laws are . . . (not) abolished."[62] It seems as if Lukács maintained simultaneously *freedom* and *determinism* of consciousness. The contradiction results from Lukács's struggle with his own ontological principles, set up for the purpose of unifying nature and social reality. The proposed synthesis lends itself to two contradictory interpretations of sociability; this, of course, was noticed by Lukács's students, and it can be summed up thus: social being-in-itself— "an objective and necessary process, independent of consciousness"— will be "merely modified by human consciousness." This explains the two contradictory interpretations of sociability, the first dominated by *necessity,* the second by the *freedom of consciousness.*[63]

We do not wish to excuse Lukács's inconsistency when we point out the *new* form of consciousness, which, on the one hand, is bound to nature when social being-in-itself is "an objective and necessary process," and, on the other hand, escapes the law of necessity and may modify this process. The *new* consciousness is the condition of sociability, the old one, though a highly developed product of matter, is still a product of matter and is determined by it. Now, Lukács may write: "without consciousness, no sociability," because sociability rises from being-in-itself to the level of being-for-itself only by attaining consciousness.

Is it to Lukács's discredit to present a Hegelian solution? This cannot be our concern, since the purpose of our analysis is to elucidate the underlying ontological principles and test the consistency of their applications. The reader of the *Ontology* will concede that the revised form of consciousness, and not Hegel, is responsible for this shift in the interpretation of social reality.

The implications of this *new* form of consciousness will be felt, as Lukács's disciples rightly noted, through the whole work, but especially in the chapter on "Alienation."

Again, we must disregard possible inconsistencies in this long work, where Lukács's fidelity to Marx is tested. We leave this issue to those who wish to try Lukács in the name of a non-existent standard of authenticity. The fact remains that ontological speculations imposed on him a standard of consistency that, at least in ontology, provides an excuse for his deviations. And his deviations seem to be most severe when he discusses alienation.

The general dissatisfaction of the disciples is so profound that they do not even quote, as they did elsewhere, specific passages from this text indicating their objections to certain solutions. Instead, they write: "We disagree with the *basic conception* of this chapter: according to it, alienation (or more precisely, alienations) is a category that applies only to individuals, i.e., it is a theoretical category of personality, but not an historical one" (p. 180). If they had followed their master in the elaboration of his ontological principles, they could have cited the *reason* for the change of Lukács's position on the problem of alienation, which took place between the time he wrote *The Young Hegel* and his monograph on *Marx* (which is already a part of the *Ontology*) and the composition of the chapter on "Alienation." This change concerns the already mentioned conception of consciousness: it is no longer an epiphenomenon, no longer under the law of necessity, hence no longer bound to suffer necessarily the general form of alienation, resulting, as Marx states, from "this consolidation of our own product into an objective power over ourselves, that goes beyond our control, frustrates our expectations, voids our calculations."[64] According to the new conception, "alienation is a phenomenon in all societies only to the extent that in them the majority of individuals live a generally alienated life" (p. 180).

The authors of the "Notes," then, blame Lukács for what is the logical outcome of his ontological principle: "As a result of the basic conception of Comrade Lukács, the struggle against alienation and the struggle against subjective projections of alienation are identified, which turns out to be equal to—and likewise we cannot agree with this—the struggle of the individual against his own alienation . . . Comrade Lukács goes so far—especially on the first point—as to state: the individual is capable of abolishing his own alienation even independently of his concrete social situation. But this can only mean the transcendence of alienation in consciousness" (p. 180).

It is surprising that the authors of the "Notes" have failed to see what has been implicit in the shifting of emphasis concerning the nature of consciousness from epiphenomenon to *non*epiphenomenon. Whether Lukács's Marxist friends like it or not, this change implies the theoretical admission that even a communist society may not be without alienation. It is in flagrant contradiction with Lukács's earlier position, but not with the "second conception" of the *Ontology*. We may, then, add that there is an evolution in Lukács's thinking, and in the positive sense, towards a greater *internal consistency,* or, if the authors of the "Notes" peer at this new development from their ideological bias, one may reply to them that Lukács's deviations are *self-explanatory.* We can even produce an answer, coming from the latest Lukács, just before his death, from the author of the *Prolegomena:* "ideologies may . . . take us closer to being as well as lead us astray."[65] Whatever be the meaning of "ideology" in this context, it universally upholds the superiority of ontology over ideologies, even over Marxist ideology; or, at least, Marxist ontology would be its highest form.

However, what may seem clear and logical in our development is blurred by other remarks in the *Ontology.* We have insisted on the fact placed before us, both by Lukács and his students, that consciousness at a certain point ceases to be an epiphenomenon. Perhaps it never was an epiphenomenon.

Lukács was forced into these concessions by what he observed of the emergence of creativity in human labor.

Now, his students, although accusing him of presenting consciousness as *nonexistent* (*not* an epiphenomenon), seem to approve of his innovation, saying: "we cannot agree to the reduction of consciousness to the reflection of reality: if consciousness were really just this reflection, how would we understand that the realization of that which is formed in consciousness produces something new?" (p. 175). We cannot blame Lukács for being inconsistent when he calls consciousness *nonexistent,* since *one* of his ontological principles, indeed his main ontological principle, the *material principle,* dictates that consciousness be *nonexistent* from the moment it is liberated form matter. The case of consciousness illustrates well how Lukács is entangled in his "theory." It illustrates also the pitfalls of his ontological thinking. It is the new ontological status of consciousness as *nonreality* that opens the way for the production of entities not deducible from nature, hence something that is not the result of reflection (*Widerspiegelung*).

We object to the Four that they never look for reasons for an interpretation in Lukács, although, as we have shown in the case of alienation, there are such reasons. Even if he did not always abide by it, Lukács learned the rule of ontology: consistency; hence his struggle with his own "convictions," and by this we mean the not always well-founded reasons, or we allude to difficulties that can be overcome only in an "ideology," for example, the dualism of soul and body. Indeed, the consequences of a consciousness that is *not* an epiphenomenon could have led to the positing of a soul as substance, as occurred in earlier ontologies. Of course, Lukács must shrink away from such pitfalls because it would be an evident denial of materialism. Hence, he affirms that "the development of biology as science produces constantly new and better arguments in favor of the inseparability of consciousness and being [*Sein*], and the impossibility of the existence of a "soul" as independent substance."[66]

Of course, if Lukács maintains this position, he has to explain also how the soul (consciousness) emerges from matter, or evolves from material conditions towards its independence from matter. Here, he has no choice but to speak of a "leap" (*Sprung*). The example we quote refers to labor and language, but both are intimately related to consciousness; we may rightly call them products of consciousness: "As in labor," writes Lukács, "also in language, a leap takes place from natural being (*Natursein*) into social being." Then follows a totally illogical explanation: "here, as there, this leap is a slow process . . . " (p. 123).[67]

Where does Lukács's inconsistency lie? A *leap* introduces an *irrational,* unexplainable element into his ontological system, hence it barely differs from what he himself calls religious ontologies, which affirm the dualism of soul and body; a slow process, on the other hand, presupposes the existence of consciousness *in potency* which is no less than the tacit admission of dualism, since *ex nihilo nihil fit.*

Lukács has no choice but to resort to this irrational element in order to make the rest of his explanation rational. Once the leap (*Sprung*) is accepted, his critique of dualism runs smoothly with the usual arguments against spiritualism, religion, idealism, and so forth. He is also assured of the necessary support to deal with men's distinctive activity — the conferring of meaning on the things and phenomena that we encounter — without falling back into the traditional way of dealing with this delicate philosophical problem, a problem that demonstrates most clearly the difference between maker and idea, nature and man, necessity and freedom. Of course, once the *"qualitative leap"* is accomplished, one may speak of what is obvious, namely, that we give meaning to our activity in such a way that these meanings cannot come under any category of nature (p. 128).

Now it is also easy to speak of philosophers who tried "honestly and with success" to purify the transcendent-theological dogma and to give new formulation to the old dualism of soul and body and to maintain the inseparability of the biological from the mental, considering the former as the indispensable foundation of the latter (p. 128).

Since our purpose is not to argue the validity of Lukács's solution for the explanation of such phenomena as language, thought, and thinking, we may conclude with his students that he often gives contradictory answers to one and the same problem; in the present case, to the problem of consciousness.[68]

Furthermore, we raise the question whether Lukács has really overcome the difficulties of "the old materialism" that intellectually compromised the movement "from below" by trying to explain complex phenomena as direct products of the less complex ones (e.g., thought as a pure product of nature). The reference (p. 91) to Marx as the founder of the new materialism (thanks to his distinction of *nature* from *society*) although holding firm to the affirmation that nature is the basis of human existence, does not seem to offer what Lukács is looking for, namely, the ontological foundation of the category of ideal beings (such as for example, thought and meaning). Let the reader decide whether Lukács's contribution to this problem — the *qualitative leap* — is a satisfactory answer to the dualism of man and nature.

Whichever be the philosophical choice of our reader, our reflections on these matters bring to the fore the fact that materialism in its old form did not satisfy Lukács, because it failed to pass the test of applicability.

His disciples sum up the "second conception of ontology," which is effectively the critique of traditional Marxism, in the following way: (1) the ontological relevance of consciousness; (2) the "Homer problem": social continuity cannot be reduced to economic development; (3) traditional Marxism replaced the alternatives by a mechanical conception of necessity; (4) the false dualism of being and consciousness in traditional Marxism.[69]

Should we mention that for an intellectual experiencing the social, cultural, and economic development of the West in the past fifty years, these shortcomings of traditional Marxism have become a fact of life? It was not necessary that they be theoretically invented or foreseen; they simply had to be noticed.

We assume that Lukács did notice these shortocmings a long time ago and that his intellectual endeavors to build a theoretical foundation of praxis are the proofs of his awareness of them. We have even affirmed that his life seems to have been devoted to the task of finding a remedy for the ills of a system of thought, and that for us this task constituted the *internal consistency* of his life.

Now, does Lukács pass the second test, which we have called the ground rule of ontology, the test of internal consistency of his proposed solution? Is the postulation of a *qualitative leap,* which is meant to explain the fundamental difference between man and nature, freedom and necessity, while upholding the basic tenet of materialism — matter as the primary principle of all beings — a more rational formulation of the problem than the one that postulates at the outset the dualism of matter and spirit (or mind and matter)? Do we not face the age-old dilemma, whatever form of philosophizing we choose? We have to abandon either the scientific foundation of ontology or busy ourselves with science while renouncing the question of the origin of being, and along with it that of values and morals, since they are bound to an ontology.

If so, then Lukács's original insight was correct: *No ethics without ontology.* But, as we have seen earlier in the chapter entitled "The Vienna Paper" and in the objections of the Budapest school, Lukács succeeds in sinning against both ontology and ideology. If we wanted to point out the irony of internal consistency in Lukács's life, we should say that this wavering between ontology and ideology is characteristic of his whole life. He rebels constantly against standards (economic, literary, philosophical, moral) but never enough to be thrown to the extreme of the opposition. His engagement cannot reach, because of his incessant compromise, the climax of *Marxist paradox,* i.e., a Marxist who would follow out his own innovations to the end, even at the risk of the collapse of his system. When his ontology forces him into compromises, such as those regarding the nature of consciousness, he shrinks back from drawing the ultimate ontological conclusion in the realm of ideology. In this way he realizes internal consistency only in fits and starts and we find only *local consistency* from the strictly ontological point of view.

However, as their objections show, the disciples do not even see this local consistency, for they do not understand the exigencies of ontology. Hence, part of their criticism is unjustified when Lukács's ontological innovations are at stake; then their objections stand only on the ground of the mixed standard — ideology and internal logic of Lukács's solutions.

The disciples have an easy victory over their teacher, since the latter constantly wavers between ontology and ideology and on this ground there is hardly any statement which he does not contradict somewhere in different contexts (as happens in the case of consciousness), under the pressure of a *local consistency.*

This criticism sounds far too severe compared to our praise of the Lukácsian venture, but we voice it anyway, not without feeling disappointment that our expectations were not fulfilled. We wished to push the implications of such an ontology to their ultimate conclusion, because we hoped to find in them, to use Lukács's students' expression, "the continuation and elaboration of *his own last philosophical intentions.*" But we are compelled to add that *internal consistency* is realized only in intention; in fact, the enterprise turns out to be a fatal *auto-destruction.*

Lukács has left behind the important fragment of a work that probably no one will continue and very few will peruse. Some of his admirers in the Marxist camp, such as Lucien Goldmann, have not taken any notice of his works beyond the period covering *History and Class Consciousness* and what followed immediately thereafter. Did Goldmann not know of the existence of this work, which was, apparently, common talk among intellectuals at the end of the 1960s? Indeed, Lukács speaks of it in interviews on several occasions. The fact remains that to express his admiration for Lukács, and to let the West know what a decisive influence the latter had on leading thinkers such as Heidegger, Goldmann totally neglects Lukács's writings after 1930, which he qualifies as belonging to the Stalinist period. Does his opinion lessen the importance of the *Ontology?*

Chapter 5   The Usefulness of the *Ontology*

We called the *Ontology* of Lukács the theory of praxis, i.e., the justification of a certain way of action. Our terminology meant to adapt itself to the Marxist problematic of theory and praxis. Those Marxists who are mainly concerned with the *changing of the world* are usually little concerned with its interpretation, which latter we called simply the justification of praxis. Current practice reveals a great diversity of views among Marxists; but these views have one characteristic in common – they are *political* views, scarcely requiring theoretical justification. For all men of action belonging to this category, the *Ontology* of Lukács is of little use, except perhaps to find occasional and vague reference in it to a phraseology common in all Marxist ideologies concerning the sociohistorical, or socioeconomic factors and to a crude form of dialectic.

For whom, then, did Lukács write the *Ontology?* The simplest answer would be: for himself, since he intended to work out a Marxist ethics and for this he required the criterion of being; or, more specifically, the criterion of social being.

Nevertheless, as all intellectuals who dialogue with themselves intend to reach out to others concerned with similar issues, Lukács's work is also written for Marxist intellectuals who are engaged in speculations about the theoretical grounds of Marxism. Here, we might list the Marxists at our universities. After all, if it is unrealistic to demand theoretical justification for his acts from the man in the street, it should not be so with intellectuals: intellectual honesty among the latter should have an effect on their thinking similar to the well-known Kantian *categorical imperative:* "Act in such a way that you may wish that your maxim of action may become a universal law." Translated into the concrete language of unviersity professors and teachers of all sorts, this law would read as follows: Teach in such a way that you may wish that your method of arguing out the "truth" about your Marxism may be turned into a universal law of professional ethics.

Again, we are faced with the same difficulty we have confronted in interpreting Lukács's life and its authenticity. Not being able to come to terms with authentic Marxism, we have proposed then the limited form of authenticity, the internal consistency of a life. Now, considered from the point of view of ethics, the internal consistency of a life can be expressed by the synonymous term, "intellectual honesty." The internal consistency of a life is translated first into intellectual honesty towards oneself; then into intellectual honesty towards others. The same idea expressed in unambiguous terms would sound similar to the hortative formulation of the categorical imperative for intellectuals: Do not mislead (indoctrinate) your listeners!

If the *Ontology* will be little used by politicians who are mainly concerned with the changing of the world, it should be the ten commandments of intellectuals. But it will also become the yardstick that measures the politicians' actions — regardless of their liking or disliking such a criterion. By saying this, I do not mean that in an ontology we find the truth, the whole truth, and nothing but the truth. I mean, rather, that an ontology is a test of consistency for any philosophy; for this reason it is obliged to spell out the first principles of a philosophy; to use a more modern formulation: it seeks the foundations of a philosophy. For this reason, it must answer even those questions that praxis is permitted to lay aside. On this assumption, ontology becomes a basis not only for comparing conflicting interpretations of reality, but also for finding similarities among doctrines. It offers a guarantee that comparisons do not turn out to be misleading.

For the sake of illustration, I take Lucien Goldmann's *Lukács et Heidegger,*[1] in which Goldmann attempts to approach the views of two philosophies on essential issues such as the relationship of subject and object, praxis, authenticity, being, and totality.

However, I must point out at the start that Goldmann takes no notice of the *Ontology*. He holds a peculiar view on Lukács's literary and philosophical production: works after 1923 belong to the Stalinist writing of Lukács. Therefore, his comparison is based on Lukács's early works *Die Seele und die Formen, "The Soul and Its Forms"* and his *History and Class Consciousness.*

When inquiring into Goldmann's intent in carrying out such a comparison, we are faced with another enigma; therefore, it will be safer simply to pose some questions. For example: who could have benefitted from such a comparison, Heidegger or Lukács? Which of them, Heidegger or Lukács, would have gained in reputation? Let us not forget, the preface of the proposed book by Goldmann dates from 1970; at that time Heidegger was certainly the more commented on and disputed author. This fact sheds light on the whole undertaking, and the chronology of the works cited in the comparison — Lukács's *History and Class Consciousness* (1923) and Heidegger's *Sein und Zeit* (1927) — decides the question. Goldmann suggests that Lukács is a kind of forerunner of Heidegger, or that the Heideggarian notions of authenticity, being, and *Vorhandenheit,* are only aspects of reification, totality, and praxis. Of course, Goldmann would not go as far as to affirm the identity of the two methods and would also maintain certain differences, but he definitely reduces the gap between the two, and, without any doubt, in favor of Lukács.

If my hypothesis is correct, the *Ontology,* or, taking this term in its broad sense, any work demonstrating an essential similarity with the *Ontology,* should serve as a touchstone to test the validity of Goldmann's allegations.

So far, I have not discussed *History and Class Consciousness* when referring to ontological issues. From *Tactics and Ethics,* I moved "arbitrarily" to the *Ontology* so that the *unity* of Lukács's work could be seen in retrospect. I avoided *History and Class Consciousness* for other reasons also: the successive condemnations of its tenets; Lukács's own autocriticism; and the complaints that enemies of Marxism took advantage of the "deviations" of this early work, wherein Lukács had not yet mastered the teaching of Marx sufficiently well to give it a correct interpretation.

Now that I am freed from these accusations, and since I am trying to counter Goldmann's arguments rather than those of Lukács, I shall take up some of the issues discussed in this work in the light of ontological principles. But again, I refuse to discuss, in this context, whether Lukács presented the authentic teaching of Marx in the first version or in the second, corrected, version, because the issue now at stake is his relationship to Heidegger.

Let us follow Goldmann's exposition of the essential resemblance between the teaching of Lukács and Heidegger, first under the heading of *man* and the *world.*

As we have seen earlier (p. 13), Lukács retracted his deviations only to confirm them in another way; hence, we may well avoid taking them into account, as does Goldmann.

First, it is hard to camouflage from any reader that Goldmann's intent in comparing some of Lukács's key notions to those of Heidegger is to boost Lukács's popularity. At first sight, considering only the terms as they appear in the text, he succeeds quite well. He even offers an explanation for Heidegger's sophisticated style compared to the relatively simple vocabulary of Lukács: Lukács had been writing for those Marxists who were not trained in philosophy: worker parties and unions.

Nevertheless, this explanation does not seem to bring Lukács closer to Heidegger. Those of us who read Lukács in German can hardly find such an explanation acceptable, for Lukács's style is rather difficult, if not clumsy. It has the characteristics of bad German academic writing; Kostas Axelos went so far as to remind Lukács in his Preface to the French translation of *History and Class Consciusness* that Lukács could also have made his autocriticism from the point of view of style. Thus, Lukács becomes more readable in translation than in the original; but even so, it is doubtful that workers and Marxist activists have ever acquired class consciousness through Lukács's writing.

On the contrary, out of Lukács's undertaking arises the greatest Marxist paradox: intellectuals, having little or no concrete connection with the working class, rather than workers, gain "class consciousness" through Lukács's writings. This fact explains Lukács's place in the academic community of the West. Goldmann's lectures on Lukács and Heidegger could not be addressed to any other than intellectual audiences, who consider themselves, in spite of their "intellectual" commitment to Marxism, as the *intelligentsia,* or the *elite,* and who expect to be the *ruling class* in a *classless* society. The other Marxist paradox is also Lukácsian in nature. Intellectuals seek justification for their commitments, and therefore Lukács's writings hold in their libraries a distinguished place. But the very same intellectuals, when facing those whom they intend to save, argue rather by means of their "examples" as Marxists, hence the *internal consistency* of their political faith is taken for granted, as if this part of Marx's teaching could not be questioned.

For this reason, the Marxism of intellectuals such as Goldmann and others must be subject to the criterion of intellectual honesty, because teaching can become the most powerful *praxis.* Being subject to the same criterion, I cannot decline, as a teacher, the obligation to oversee Goldmann's teaching with regard to Lukács and his relationship to Heidegger, and to demonstrate the applicability of my thesis on a concrete example.

Goldmann, Lukács, and Heidegger

How shall we approach the criticism of Goldmann's interpretation in his book *Lukács and Heidegger?* After all, Goldmann is not an ordinary party member; his knowledge of philosophy should certainly be a guarantee of his objectivity. Nevertheless, the reader is soon served warning of Goldmann's bias, as evidenced by Marixst phraseology such as "history is not reserved for the elite as in *Sein und Zeit"* (p. 108). Or to instance another bold statement: "There is no fundamental difference between the positions of Heidegger and the Theses on Feuerbach in which knowledge is always bound to a praxis" (p. 104).

Goldmann does not seem to realize that if he insists on the fact that there is no fundamental difference between the positions of Heidegger and the Theses on Feuerbach, he cannot speak either of essential differences between Heidegger and Lukács.

The fundamental identity of Heidegger and Lukács seems to concern the foundation of foundations, Being in Heidegger and Totality in Lukács. "What

Heidegger tells us about the category of Being, was already in Lukács's notion of totality" (p. 106).

Let us first examine this assumption before going any further in the analysis of Goldmann's thesis asserting the fundamental identity of the two philosophies.

Hegel might have provided a common denominator in terms of which to compare totality and Being, since both Lukács and Heidegger owe a great deal to him. Indeed, *Ganzheit* (totality) is a Hegelian term. But, can Lukács mean the same as Hegel, if Hegel's philosophy is, as he claimed, a materialism turned upside down?

Of course, *Sein* (Being) is also a kind of totality, but a *totality of a different order.* In saying this, we enter the realm of ontology: we may all speak about the same things, we may even take as our starting point *everyday life (Alltäglichkeit)* — Heidegger and Lukács did so — without arriving at the same conclusion concerning the *nature* of these phenomena.

The usefulness of ontology lies, as we have said, in its determination to reach the bottom of things (beings), and to spell out in unambiguous terms — I mean, without jargon, which encompasses such worn-out expressions as "socioeconomic," "sociocultural," and the rest — the *nature of reality*. Or, if the term "nature" is shocking to some, we may say the *"essence"* of reality.

Now, let us ask the question, "What is the essence of reality for Lukács?" since his "totality" must necessarily be of the same nature. Lukács always reaffirmed his materialism by referring directly to Marx, as if he wanted to proclaim his otherwise doubtful fidelity to his master. Now, if the first principle of reality is matter, totality must also be conceived as *some kind* of material totality. This fact has far-reaching consequences for an ontology. For if it is so, all changes affecting this totality and all changes affecting man as part of this totality are bound to some form of *causality,* acting *through* and *in* the concrete. We find on the very first page of Lukács's *Ontology,* dealing with historical questions, the following remark: "Social being has several domains and all of them seem to be subject to the same kind of necessity and order of laws as nature itself."[2]

Hence, *being-in-the-world,* rather than *facing the world,* which Goldmann considered as a great innovation of Lukács, has to be viewed in terms of causality. But that would be unacceptable to Heidegger. For us, who seek the ultimate ground for being, and also a comparison between philosophers using similar vocabulary, the decisive concern is not Goldmann's assertion that both Heidegger and Lukács sought the abolition of the traditional subject–object dualism, but rather the underlying principles that allow the phasing out of this dualism.

Now, could we assert that this ground is *causality* for both Heidegger and Lukács?

It is obvious that no Marxist would ever conceive reality otherwise than under the category of causality. What would become of dialectical materialism, if causality were excised from the system? Hence, causality is undoubtedly an ontological principle for Lukács and for Marxism in whatever guise they choose to represent it to themselves.

Now, for a phenomenologist, *causality* as a presupposition goes against his presuppositionless philosophy. There is no causality of Being in Heidegger, though there is in Thomas Aquinas's ontology. It is easy to verify in Heidegger that the *destruction* of metaphysics was necessary to eliminate the old type of ontology in which Being could be called "First Cause" or "Highest Being."

This essential difference between Being and Totality rules out any comparison on this matter between Lukács and Heidegger. Therefore, we will not pursue further the interpretation of Being in Heidegger. However, we may add to the debate an additional fact — without demonstration — concerning the ontology of Heidegger: "The being that exists is man. Man alone exists. Rocks are, but they do not exist. Trees are, but they do not exist . . . The proposition "man alone exists" does not mean . . . that man alone is a real being while all other beings are unreal."[3] Probably such statements prompted Lukács to give Heidegger the title "bourgeois philosopher," since he had the time to waste for such nonsense.

But let us pursue our comparison now on the basis of this new discovery, the essential difference between Being and Totality, and ask ourselves how man (for Lukács) and *Dasein* or Being-there (for Heidegger) relate to Totality and Being? According to Goldmann, the terminology makes no essential difference, since both, Lukács and Heidegger, refer to man. By saying this Goldmann qualifies Heidegger's innovation (*Dasein,* instead of man) as a fancy of Heidegger's imagination, and overlooks the intent of this terminology in the description of man's being-in-the-world and especially its relationship to Totality or Being. The meaning of *Dasein,* properly understood, excludes *Dasein*'s relationship to a Totality governed by causality. Such a totality would interfere with *Dasein's* freedom, which is, in Heidegger's philosophy (at least in that of the "first" Heidegger, as it is customary to call him), limited to the *interpretation of the world* (hermeneutics) rather than being instrumental in *changing* the world. Strictly speaking, *Dasein* has the power to choose itself (to be authentic) or not to choose itself (to be inauthentic). Man or *Dasein* could fulfill just the first part of Marx's eleventh thesis on Feuerbach, it could only interpret the world. That someone could move from the interpretation of the world toward the changing of the world is not excluded by the Heideggerian definition of man, but even if *Dasein* did so, Heidegger's definition forces him to look for a model elsewhere than in the dialectics of history understood in the Marxian way. In sum, the basic rule of hermeneutics is to ask the author (or a text) what question this author intended to answer. Heidegger gave a clear statement of his intent on the first page of *Sein und Zeit:* "Die konkrete Ausarbeitung der Frage nach dem Sinn von *"Sein"* ist die Absicht der folgenden Abhandlung."[4]

The definition of man as *Dasein,* and Heidegger's intention of working out in the concrete the question concerning the meaning of being, *determine* the role of such terms as *in-der-Welt-sein* (being-in-the-world) and their elaboration. First of all, the world is not the totality, and the abolition of the distinction between subject and object has not been introduced to correct a subjectivist deviation à la Descartes and Kant or to stress the *interaction* of the world and man-in-the-world. Interaction in Lukács is a way of stressing how the two, world and man, shape each other. This is not at all the case with *Dasein.* The titles of some chapters in *Sein und Zeit* should clarify our assertion: "Being-in-the-world in general as the basic state of *Dasein;*" "Being-in-the-world as Being-with and Being-one's-self." They indicate the very direction of *Dasein's* movement: from the Being-in-the-world *in general,* to *Being-one's-self.* This itinerary of *Dasein* towards itself (the Self) should be taken only as an intermediate stage along with many others, such as care, Being-towards-death, and temporality as means in the expression of the meaning of Being (*Sinn von Sein*). Why, then, stress the world and Being-in-the world as essential in the understanding of Being? In a rather schematic way, which nevertheless does not distort Heidegger's teaching, we may say that, on the one hand, *Dasein* is the *link* between *Sein* and *Seiende* (beings, entities), and on the other hand, *Sein* has no definition and all attempts to elaborate the meaning of *Sein* therefore pass through entities (*Seiende*), hence the *concrete elaboration* of the meaning of *Sein.*

Goldmann singled out *possible* similarities in Heidegger and Lukács. Such an undertaking involves a risk far too great for both philosophies, for it has to reduce them to a common denominator to render the comparison *possible.* For Goldmann, in order to succeed in this venture, and to such an extent that he would be taken seriously among those who are familiar with these philosophies, there should have been not only a common *ground (Grund)* prior to all terminology but also a common *purpose* contemplated by the two philosophers. Our analysis has shown that Goldmann failed to prove that Being and Totality are of the same nature. It does not rule out that the two philosophers might have had, at the outset of their investigations, the same purpose. So far as Heidegger's intent is concerned, it is clearly spelled out on

the first page of his *Sein und Zeit.* His method is also specified: "Die Interpretation der Zeit als das mögliche Horizont eines jeden Seinsverständnisses
überhaupt . . . [5]

If Heidegger's intent was to elaborate in a concrete way the meaning of
Being (*Sein*), we may interpret his sentence as follows: this elaboration has to
take the form of an analysis that involves the *experience* of a being, in Heidegger's case, *Dasein,* as it is related to Being, i.e., to *Sein.* The locus of this experience is also indicated: it is the *horizon of time.* What is not spelled out at
the outset, but becomes evident as soon as the analysis begins, is that the *time*
involved is the *internal time of consciousness.* We could then say, without
distorting Heidegger's philosophy, that the horizon where *Sein* had to appear
is the horizon of consciousness; since consciousness can mark the unfolding of
events only in succession or simultaneity and not in extension, i.e., in space,
those characteristics must determine the unfolding of the meaning of *Sein*
(*Sinn von Sein*) in *Time.* Nevertheless, there is something that stands for *extension,* and this is the intensity of experience that can be translated into the well-
known expressions "authenticity" and "inauthenticity." Do we exaggerate or distort Heidegger's philosophy in saying that history and historicality also belong to
the internal time sequence of consciousness? If this can be maintained, and
there is no reason why it could not, in the light of the main objective, the concrete elaboration of the meaning of *Sein (Being), Heidegger's Dasein,* in spite
of its concreteness and involvement in Time, is *man of all times,* hence, an
ahistorical phenomenon. Such a *man* has no place in Lukács's interpretation
of *class consciousness* or *reification and the consciousness of the proletariat.*

If our presupposition is correct, Heidegger's *Dasein* can raise itself to
authenticity or decline into inauthenticity under any social, economic, or
political system. The condition of authenticity depends *on the individual alone*
because it consists in the interiorization of the relationship with Being (*Sein*)
and not in the realization of a form of exchange of goods and production that
curtails *reification. Reification,* on the other hand, as Lukács explains it, is
bound to history, to *Geschichte,* in the sense in which this term is used by
Heidegger, and that is a *chronological sequence of events that excludes repetition* (i.e., physical sequence of historical events).

Our purpose is not to decide whether Engels, Marx, or Lukács was right,
but to show that for each of them history was a chain of events and causes,
whereas in Heidegger's philosophy those terms that have ontological
significance, namely, "historicality" (*"Geschichtlichkeit"*) and "historical"
(*"geschichtlich"*, do not imply causality. This doctrine is in line with *Dasein*'s
ahistorical character, which Lukács has also noticed. Therefore, when Heidegger speaks of history (*"Geschichte"*), he uses this term with a connotation
which would be unacceptable to Marxists.

Heidegger discusses the various significations of history (*Geschichte*), then raises numerous questions: "Does *Dasein* first become historical (*geschichtlich*) by getting intertwined with events and circumstances? Or is the Being of Dasein constituted first of all by historizing, so that anything like circumstances, events and vicissitudes is ontologically possible only *because Dasein is historical* (*geschichtlich*) in its Being?" Then, the very meaning of history is revealed through *Dasein's historicality*. Heidegger goes so far as to state that "the existential–ontological constitution of historicality (*Geschichtlichkeit*) is covered up by the way *Dasein*'s history (*Geschichte*) is ordinarily interpreted."[6]

Would it not be right to say that *history* as Lukács understood it is an impediment in the way of understanding the meaning of Being (*Sinn von Sein*) and the Being of *Dasein*?

Again, we encounter a paradox, not unusual in Heidegger's philosophy of Being: the *ahistorical Dasein* is *historical* in its Being, therefore intertwined with events and circumstances. On this ground, *Dasein* can respond to these events and circumstances authentically or inauthentically and its historicality unfolds in these responses. "It becomes plain that *Dasein*'s inauthentic historicality (*Geschichtlichkeit*) lies in that which—under the title of "everydayness"—we have looked upon, in the existential analytic of *Dasein,* as the horizon that is closest to us."[7]

The subtlety of Heidegger's terminology is easily overlooked when only superficial similarity is taken for the ground of comparison. The importance of meaning (*Sinn*) always takes precedence in Heidegger over the historical character of an event. Thus, for example, technic is a social form of activity in the common acceptation of this term, and on this ground, it is bound to history. However, its essence is revealed or covered up by *Dasein*'s historicality authentically or inauthentically *in time,* but *in any time* of human history. In sum, *historicality* (*Geschichtlichkeit*) does not imply the dialectic nature of history, that is its necessities and order of laws that are independent of man. Historicality belongs to the Being of man.

Now it becomes evident that this distinction makes the comparison between Lukács and Heidegger hazardous.

However, does it also mean that Lukács's analysis of reification loses its validity? Not at all. It is true, but on another level than that of the analysis of *Dasein* in Heidegger. I am tempted to use a Marxist term to situate its validity. It could be said that it is true on the level of economic superstructure. Lukács's notion of reification is based on the laws of the exchange of goods and their relationship to labor, out of which emerges Marx's notion of fetishism, evidently with some difference: Lukács's innovation is the claim that *reifica-*

tion leads to alienation on the social and individual level. Here again, should we not ask what is the subject that undergoes alienation?

Goldmann admits that there is a difference between the conception of subject in Lukács and Heidegger. "The real subject of any historical action," for Lukács, who borrows from Marx here, "the subject of all human actions is 'un sujet pluriel' ('a subject in the plural'),"[8] whereas in Heidegger we deal with an *individual subject*. Goldmann refers to this difference as if it proved Lukács's superiority over Heidegger; perhaps because this difference explains why a whole class of society, such as the working class, is subject to alienation based on alienated labor.

Nevertheless, we may now call it a fact that history itself contradicted Lukács; the abolition of reification on the social level does not necessarily lead to the abolition of alienation on the individual level. At this point Goldmann's distinction between collective subject and individual subject, cited as the essential difference between Lukács and Heidegger, reveals the superiority of Heidegger, rather than his shortcomings. The *Ontology* would have informed Goldmann of Lukács's difficulties in coping with *reification* and *objectivation* on the individual level. It is in the *Ontology,* under the pressure of the principles of relatedness and internal consistency, that Lukács admits suddenly that human consciousness is *not* an epiphenomenon like animal consciousness, and abandons, as his disciples noted, *Widerspiegelung* (reflection) as a means of overcoming alienation.[9] Are these factors not indications that Lukács retracted his previous views? This is the admission that the collective subject is not sufficient to explain reification and alienation. A revised notion of *freedom* is needed to explain the individual differences, out of which emerges the *individual* encounter with the problem of alienation through the interiorization of the world and its projection.

The great artistic achievements alluded to by Lukács in the Vienna paper[10] are exceptions to the "general rule" of reification and alienation, and to the rules of false consciousness; the idea of the plural subject does not apply to them. We may safely affirm that the requirements for internal consistency forced Lukács to change the presupposition which he still retained in *Tactics and Ethics.* This essay professes, if not explicitly, certainly implicitly, *collective freedom* as ground for the acts of the terrorist. But as I noted in my analysis of it, there is no *collective* freedom, or there is no "transindividual subject," in Goldmann's terms:[11] that would be a form of "false consciousness," to use Lukács's own terminology. Even class consciousness is possible only on the assumption that human consciousness is not an epiphenomenon, and is not transindividual.

These elements, which enable us to make a comparison between Lukács and Heidegger, are scattered throughout the *Ontology* and often obscured in prolixity. This is the reason I consider the Vienna paper a daring adventure as compared to the overly long *Ontology,* because in this "summary" the internal consistency and inconsistency of the work become readily visible.

Basic Differences Determine Differences in Details: Zuhandenheit, Vorhandenheit, and Praxis

The usefulness of the *Ontology* is further demonstrated in the examination of other aspects of the two philosophies, which, though not central, are, in an ontological outlook, integral parts of a whole, and hence dependent on the basic *ontological principle.* We recall that this principle was, for Lukács, matter.

This time, Goldmann borrows in his comparison of Lukács and Heidegger two notions from Heidegger that seem to be essential for both in spite of the differences of approach and the difference in the order of priorities. These notions are *Zuhandenheit* ("readiness-to-hand") and *Vorhandenheit* ("presence-at-hand"). The two are brought by Goldmann under one common denominator — praxis — and this suggests to Goldmann a conclusion favoring Lukács over Heidegger on the treatment of instruments (in the hands of man) and things of nature (at the disposal of man).

Earlier, speaking of Being and Totality in the two philosophies, Goldmann stressed their *identiy.* In the case of *Zuhandene* and *Vorhandene,* he speaks of an essential difference. If our assumption, that the ontological principle governs the internal consistency of a philsophy, is correct, then Goldmann is in contradiction with himself. This means that fundamental identity excludes essential differences even in the details. At best it allows minor differences in approach to the problems; in this case, to the problem of entities categorized under *presence-at-hand* and *readiness-to-hand.*

We also wish to stress that the "essential difference" in dealing with certain issues does not by itself imply the superiority of one philosophy over the other. In this specific case, with regard to *Vorhandene* and *Zuhandene,* the difference is essential, indeed, between Lukács and Heidegger, but for reasons other than those mentioned by Goldmann. The arguments of the two do not follow the same *ontological* path. Rendered in the technical language of Heidegger: Lukács's reflections move on the *ontic* level, and Heidegger's on the *ontological* level. Now, this difference means very little to someone who refuses to admit that philosophy could have as its only preoccupation *Being,* and *Being as such,* and nothing else, or rather Nothingness as Being. But for Heidegger the distinction between *ontic* and *ontological, Seiende* and *Sein,* constitutes the ground (*Grund*) for philosophizing. Heidegger clearly states that the problem of *Zuhandenheit* is only part of his overall preoccupation, voiced in the question, "What is Being?" *Zuhandene* and *Vorhandene* are his preoccupations as *Seiende* (entities) that *Dasein* encounters in his surrounding and whose *Being* is at issue for *Dasein* and not their *ontic* status as *instrument* or *thing.* Hence it is not the *praxis* of man, as man fashioning his world, which is Heidegger's concern. For Heidegger's *Dasein* the world is *there,* it is already *made,* what is required is that it be *understood,* i.e., *interpreted,* which is exactly what is forbidden by the second half of the famous eleventh thesis on Feuerbach.

Interpretation can mean the type of approach Lukács uses in his *interpretation* of *reification,* which would take us back again into the justified comparison advocated by Goldmann. Let us recall, therefore, the distinction Heidegger introduced into ontological speculations. We would insist on this fact, neither to stress the subtlety of Heidegger's language, nor, as does Goldmann, to excuse the more straightforward style of Lukács. For Heidegger the *ontic* level is the level of science where *causality* and *necessity* reign; whatever praxis is pursued on this level, it will never totally eliminate the dualism of subject and object, fact and value, since this dualism is the precondition of science, and, we may add, it is also the precondition of the Marxist dialectic.

Goldmann sees the *superiority* of Marxist thought over Heidegger's in this dialectic (p. 100), but in this case, he should also abandon the so-called abolition of subject–object dualism, which, according to him, Lukács intended to bring about. Furthermore, Marxist dialectic functions on the precondition of the "collective subject," another fact that places the argument on the *ontic* level. Will Goldmann's interpretation change the level of argument? For Marxism, writes Goldmann:

> if the world is object, the subject itself is object and the object subject. The whole historical world, at a given moment, is constituted materially and intellectually by collective subjects that can be conceived only by a science which is both dialectical and philosophical. The world is a meaningful universe which men have created and in which they live; hence men and the universe are strictly related. The relation between man and the world has two aspects: the subject is part of the world and infuses meaning into the world through praxis (pratiquement), but this world is part of the subject, and it constitutes the subject. This circle is a vicious circle only for a static philosophy, it poses no problem for a dialectical science of history. In his theses on Feuerbach, Marx says that conditions create men, but in these given conditions, men create new conditions, and

in their praxis while transforming themselves, they also transform the world [p. 100].

There is hardly any doubt, when we examine Goldmann's terminology, that Goldmann leans on Heidegger's criticism of traditional ontology, the ontology of subject and object, and has to draw support, in this way, for Lukács, who admittedly had the same intention: to overcome the traditional dualism of object and subject, fact and value. Andrew Feenberg states rightly in his article *"Reification and the Antimonies of Socialist Thought"* that "as Lukács went from the university to the Party, he found himself confronted within the socialist movement with a whole series of philosophical problems which he had already encountered in the course of his bourgeois studies . . . But unlike the philosophers of the Second International, Lukács saw in Marxism the solution to the problems of earlier philosophy, and not *vice-versa.*"[12]

One may say that Heidegger's intention was similar to that of Lukács, both to overcome the subject–object dualism essential in earlier philosophies and to overcome the *reification of consciousness* that follows inevitably from this dualism. Nevertheless, for Heidegger this objective was only part of a more fundamental issue, the question of *Being*. Hence, for him the dualism of subject–object stood in the way of understanding Being, rather than the other way around.

Since the objectives of the philosophies are not the same, it is pointless to speak of their essential identity. The difference is not a difference in vocabulary, as Goldmann tries to make out, but a fundamental difference in the approach to Being (*Sein*). These remarks should not be interpreted as the downgrading of Marxism with regard to Heidegger. I only wish to set the record straight: *the reification of consciousness* that is mentioned at two points in *Sein und Zeit* (at the beginning and at the end) can hardly be a reference to Lukács, as Goldmann tries to insinuate. I am inclined to say, and categorically, that Heidegger is not referring to Lukács at all when he mentions the *reification of consciousness.* Let us cite one of the passages alluded to by Goldmann. "It has long been known that ancient ontology works with 'thing-concepts' *(Dingbegriffen)* and there is a danger of 'reifying consciousness,' " writes Heidegger at page 437 of *Sein und Zeit.* Then he adds: "Why does this reifying always keep coming back to exercise its dominion? What positive structure does the Being of 'consciousness' have, if reification remains inappropriate to it? Is the 'distinction' between 'consciousness' and 'thing' sufficient for tackling the ontological problematic in a primordial manner?"

If this passage were a direct reference to Lukács, as Goldmann suggests — adducing in support of his contention the fact that the term "reification of consciousness" (*Verdinglichung des Bewusstseins*) is in quotation marks — it should be considered as a severe ciriticsm of Lukács's interpretation of *reification*. Do we not read in Heidegger that the distinction between "consciousness" and "thing" is insufficient to tackle the ontological problematic in a primordial manner, since we do not even know what this "reifying" signifies or where it arises. Would it not be strange on the part of Heidegger to refer to Lukács by either approving of his treatment of reification or disapproving of it, when he admits not knowing exactly in what the reification of consciousness consists? But even if that were the case, there is another insurmountable difficulty in the way of dealing with the issue, since "can we even seek the answer as long as the *question* of the meaning of Being remains unformulated and unclarified?"[13] Heidegger's text seems to indicate clearly that he addresses himself to the problem of reification in regard to the problem of Being and not with reference to Lukács. Hence, even if Lukács could be considered a forerunner of Heidegger on the question of reification, the distance between the two approaches would not diminish. Since *Being* as such constitutes no problem for Lukács, he could not have sought the solution to reification in the way Heidegger does. Thus, even if Heidegger had found it necessary to criticize or approve of Lukács's notion of reification, he probably would have noted only, as he did for the philosophy of his time, speaking generally and not singling out anyone in particular, that *Lukács has not raised the question of Being,* and, what is more, that his philosophy is incapable of raising it; indeed, that it *conceals Being.* We all know that such an appreciation would not have made the comparison between Lukács and Heidegger easier.

Finally, it is Goldmann himself who rules out even the possibility of any essential similarity between Heidegger and Lukács, when he writes: "the whole historical world, at a given moment, is constituted materially and intellectually by collective subjects, that can be conceived only by a science which is both dialectic and philosophic" (p. 100).

In Heidegger, there is no question of the *material* or *intellectual* constitution of the universe, because that would imply a *causality.* The action of the subject on the world, and vice versa, of which Goldmann and Marx speak, is indeed *causal;* on the other hand, causality presupposes the dualism of the agent and its object, and not their *identity;* inversion of the roles, subject–object, object–subject is only inverting the *direction of causality.* It does not abolish causality. How could it, since *materialism is unthinkable without causality,* and dialectical materialism is no exception. Furthermore, it must also be true that man cannot be conceived in such systems otherwise than as subject to causality. The well-known thesis of *Widerspiegelung* that consciousness is determined through the material world follows from this state of affairs.

Now, if Lukács, in his *Ontology,* reaffirms his belief that *matter is the principle of all reality,* then he must accommodate causality, as indeed he does.

Praxis, or interaction of subject and object, is not the abolition of their dualism in the Heideggerian sense. On the other hand, one has to be cautious with the notion of identity of object and subject even in Heidegger. It makes sense only in the search for the meaning of Being (*Sinn von Sein*), where representational thinking (*das vorstellende Denken*) leads to conceptualization and in so doing proves itself inadequate to the expression of *Being,* which is not a concept.

Indeed, it is *representational thinking* that leads to *reification,* or at least to a form of reification — to the *conceptual* freezing of experience (*die begriffliche Erstarrung des Erlebens;* cf. *Was ist Metaphysik?*)[14] That could be called the reification of consciousness in the Heideggerian sense: to put it less boldly, I think Heidegger's philosophy does not exclude this interpretation, since Heidegger himself reminds us that ancient philosophy (at its height) was captive to its own *ontic* approach to things, and, because of this approach, "the specifically 'pragmatic' character of the *pragmata* is just what the Greeks left in obscurity; they thought of these 'proximally' as 'mere Things.' "[15] Thus, if we "theorize" about the emergence of such things as "instruments" (*Zuhandene*) — this is always *representational thinking,* since all theorization is carried out on this level — we shall never understand what *Zuhandenheit* (instrumentality or readiness-to-hand) is.[16] What Heidegger calls "concernful" dealing with these instruments cannot be equated either with the Marxian or Lukácsian *praxis,* because "*Besorgen*" is not a practical praxis, which is to say, it is not a preoccupation which is *representational* preoccupation. Let us not forget that Lukács solves the problem of reification of consciousness on the epistemological level, that is, on the representational level. If it were otherwise, his praxis would never lead to class consciousness, and who can deny that this is the ultimate end of Lukács's philosophy, at least as it appears in the title of his book *History and Class Consciousness.*

Heidegger suggests — not explicitly, indeed, but in the manner of an *Ungedachte* (unthought thought) — that the reification of consciousness is the result of *representational thinking* that operates with *Dingbergriffen.* I called this interpretation the *Ungedachte* of Heidegger, since it is compatible with his main doctrine, the doctrine about the meaning of Being. If representational thinking conceals Being, one has to wonder if there is a way, proper to the nature of Being, that would be considered appropriate for the thinking of Being. Heidegger proposes in his little work — *What is Metaphysics? — das andenkende Denken,* which is a way of thinking Being different from *repre-*

tational thinking: a thinking that goes around entities and grasps the meaning of their Being.[17]

It is important to stress the difference between the approaches to *pragmata,* i.e., to things, in these two forms of thinking, because it also reveals the essential difference between Lukács and Heidegger, which goes far beyond the similarity of terms—e. g., *reification of consciousness*—and originates in the basic ontological principles of the two philosophers—matter, for Lukács; Being, for Heidegger. To further develop the distinction it must be said that Lukács's thinking, in spite of his efforts to overcome the dualism of subject and object, remains a *representational* thinking (*vorstellende Denken*); and Lukács cannot do otherwise, because *causal relationships* that affect nature and society cannot be thought of in any other way. *Class consciousness* is equally bound to the representation of social reality and to the projection of this image into the social praxis of individuals. There again, individuals *representing themselves* as part of a class enduring the same way of life, hence representing themselves as a *collective subject* facing another social (collective) and physical (material) reality remain inevitably in the dualism of the subject–object relation that is the ground for representational thinking.

Goldmann confirms our assertion that only representational thinking operates in *History and Class Consciousness* by saying that "the proletariat (i.e., a collective subject) is the only social group capable of abolishing reification and capable of achieving a nonreified consciousness" (p. 93). This would mean that an individual conceived as *Dasein* according to the Heideggerian philosophy could never be able to achieve that very same goal and could never become a self (*Selbst*), which is, in the Heideggerian sense, equivalent to a *nonreified consciousness.*

Is it not clear that there is an irreconcilable difference between the two philosophies? And, with the introduction of the *andenkende Denken* by Heidegger, the gap continues to widen, since not only Being, but also entities, the pragmata, must be thought *without concepts,* which means: they must not be made into objects in the traditional sense. This way of thinking is possible only if we think the *Being of pragmata* (entities). The thinking begins by "thinking" these entities not as *instruments* (*Zuhandene*) but as *present-at-hand* (*Vorhandene*). Does it not exclude praxis in the Lukácsian sense? For Lukács the *meaning* of the *world,* the meaning of *totality,* comes from instrumentality, that is, from human praxis (*Zuhandenheit*). For Heidegger, the *meaning* of *Being* comes form the naked reality, from *Vorhandenheit,* from the mere being-there of things and their nearness to *Dasein,* or rather from *Dasein's Mitsein (being-with these entities).* This form of thinking is at the antipode of dialectical materialism because it is at the antipode of causal relation with the world. It could never lead to *class consciousness,* but only to the consciousness of the self, of course of our individual self (*Selbst*). In this *Mitsein* (being-with) there is no *interaction of subject and object,* but only *togetherness* in such a way that the *presence of the object would meet with the presence* of the subject and the two would constitute what Heidegger calls "*Anwesen*" or "parousia," a kind of presensing of the thing which is the Being of that thing. Hence, the common denominator which brings entities (*Seiende*) under the domination of man would not be praxis, which is, after all, an action, but rather an *inner experience* of subject and object, the highest form of selfhood (*Selbstheit*), which cannot become class conscious.

Goldmann quotes Heidegger, but he refuses to see why Heidegger is puzzled when he asks: "Why does Being get 'conceived' 'proximally' in terms of the present-at-hand (*Vorhandene*) *and not* in terms of the ready-to-hand (*Zuhandene*) which indeed lies *closer* to us?"[18] The *reason* is indeed specified, a few lines before the quotation that Goldmann singles out to support *his* interpretation of the similarity of the two philosophies, and especially the originality of Lukács as "recognized" by Heidegger. The *ultimate* aim of *Sein und Zeit* is not to exhibit the constitution of *Dasein*'s Being (*die Herstellung der Seinsverfassung des Daseins*). The exhibiting of the constitution of *Dasein*'s Being *is only a way,* a way towards the exhibiting of the *meaning of Being,* which is the ultimate *end* (*Ziel*); all other analyses, such as *Dasein*'s fundamental possibilities of choosing an authentic or inauthentic existence, are only stages *on the way* towards this ultimate end.

Is it not obvious that when the ultimate end of the two philosophers is not the same, the outcome of their analysis of the details cannot be, *even accidentally,* the same? What looks alike can be fundamentally different. And this fundamental difference will inevitably surface when the end results of the two philosophies have to be applied to concrete examples, that is, when ontological principles are used for the interpretation of phenomena. Such difficulties surface in the Vienna paper and are related to individual differences that remain, according to Lukács's ontological principles, inexplicable.

On the other hand, the 'ontic,' that is, the scientific approach to the phenomenon of reification, has also its strong side: it correctly explains *social injustices* and their consequences on a large scale; but we must specify: always in the context of *reciprocal causality.*

Hence the alienation of which Lukács speaks is the social alienation of rights, synonymous with the social degradation of individuals fallen victims of an economic mechanism. It is also correct that the evolution of labor–capital relations leads to the disintegration of earlier forms of society, producing disastrous consequences for families and individuals. However, one must raise the question whether a more "favorable" transformation of economic relations would not have provoked the same consequences on the level of individual and family life as were created by the so-called reification of labor: the dissolution of family and social ties is not prevented by a system that declares the proletariat "in principle" the owner of the means of production, and, we may add, it does not do away with alienation on the individual level. And, after all, is it not the alienation of man from himself which is the generic form of alienation?

Furthermore, Lukács's theory explaining "collective" alienation, as we may call it, is unable to account for individual differences in attitudes towards a state of affairs, alienation of certain rights, certain aspects of freedom, very often necessitated by the organization of state. By stressing the role of the economic order in the shaping of alienation, one must necessarily stress technological progress and consider technology as a means towards the liberation of man through the establishment of his domination over nature.

The late Lukács must have been aware of this shortcoming of the "Marxist man" because in his *Ontology,* in the chapter on "Entfremdung" ("Alienation"), he omitted *Widerspiegelung* ("reflection"), as a means for overcoming alienation. His disciples—Heller, Márkus, Fehér, and Vajda—noticed the omission. However, unable to understand the theoretical importance of this omission, they urged their master to reinstate *Widerspiegelung;* Lukács did not accede to their request and declined their help in carrying out the revision.

The disciples could not see the internal consistency of Lukács's correction: if human consciousness is *not* an *epiphenomenon* its way of knowing cannot be reflection (*Widerspiegelung*), since now consciousness has gained its independence form matter, that is, from its causal and strict determinism. Although it would be an outrageous exaggeration to claim that man, being declared something else than epiphenomenon, has become a "spiritual being" freed "totally" from nature, it is certainly possible to attribute to this "liberated" consciousness more freedom and more possibility to initiate an authentic, that is, an individual, life, than to its predecessor, the epiphenomenon.

The new "vision" of man intends to restore to man not only his individual freedom, but also an initiative that necessarily shores the foundation of culture or superstructure; it also attempts, where possible, to allow for individual differences. Such a far-reaching account is ruled out under the laws of *Widerspiegelung.*

If we look for similarity between Lukács and Heidegger, we should perhaps turn to these "fragments" of innovations found in the *Ontology.* But in that case, will we not be compelled to admit that it was not Lukács who influenced Heidegger, but more likely just the opposite? Let us just glance at *Dasein* and the possibility one has of choosing in spite of generally unfavorable conditions, an *authentic* existence, and of projecting one's life ahead of oneself in a cultural form that is, first of all, a *meaning* (which is *interpretation* of the world). This is possible only for an *individual subject* endowed with freedom.

Let us recall here Lukács's last-minute revision of the notion of man. This part of his "autocriticism" can hardly be stressed enough. Earlier, human consciousness had to be considered for reasons of doctrinal consistency — such as the role of *Widerspiegelung* in the theory of knowledge, and in the theory of artistic creation — an *epiphenomenon,* so that it could *correctly reflect reality* and ward off the temptation of false consciousness and false ideologies. Since our objective is not the criticism of *Widerspiegelung,* we simply note how Lukács made an about-face and exempted human consciousness from following the *general law* for the emergence of living being endowed with senses and consciousness. Hence Lukács's all-important *revision* of his earlier position, with the further explanation: *human consciousness is not an epiphenomenon.* Had Goldmann taken notice of this seemingly unimportant and modest statement, he would have revised his views on the relationship of Heidegger and Lukács, especially his assertions on the *plural subject* and on the main tenets of *History and Class Consciousness* concerning nonreified consciousness. Of course, Lukács did not have time to develop his thoughts in line with this last revision, but it is this, if anything, that could have brought him closer to Heidegger: for whom *Dasein,* i.e., man, is defined simply as having characteristics such as *verstehende Befindlichkeit* and *Sprache;* that is, a sort of affectivity that is coupled with understanding, the capability of language, and the possibility to choose itself, i.e., to choose authentic existence. All other characteristics and aspirations that may belong to *Dasein* are to be discovered with the help of those primordial qualities. The same task would have fallen to Lukács on the ground of his revision of the origin of consciousness, had his life not been cut short.

Lukács was aware of the shortcomings of his own ontology, and, in general, of Marxist ontology. His attempt to present human beings as "responding" beings was perhaps meant to remedy these shortcomings. Nevertheless, this "answering" is taken again in the *causal* context of labor, which in Lukács's framework immediately becomes social labor. But this explains why the *social subject* (or *plural subject*) remains the victim of reification and alienation in spite of the *socially nonreified* labor in countries where the so-called *Marxist praxis* should have rendered reification inoffensive and alienation nonexistent.

On the other hand, the Heideggerian approach to Being, and the intermediate but essential role of *Dasein* and its possibilities ("Höher als die Wirklichkeit steht die *Möglichkeit*")[19] of choosing self or nonself does not exclude social reform or social justice. This latter possibility is not vitiated by the singular subject while the qualitative expression or difference is rendered unsuccessful if the interpretation has to run through the agency of a plural subject, for example, through the agency of a class, such as the proletariat.

Ontological principles carry a number of implications that inevitably follow from the fundamental position if the internal consistency of a doctrine is to be maintained. But since Lukács did not have time to follow out the implications of his *revision* or did not foresee at that moment its tremendous impact on the doctrine, we limit our speculations to some questions that inevitably arise from the new position, and we ask ourselves how they affect the solution of the problems under discussion, here the dualism of subject and object and the order of priority in the interpretation of *Zuhandene* (ready-to-hand) and *Vorhandene* (present-at-hand). By order of priorities I mean: which of these entities comes first in the interpretation of praxis and in the understanding of Being.

Readiness-to-hand can be translated as *instrument,* i.e., the hammer in the hand of man. This example is used by Heidegger and taken up later by Goldmann to bring Heidegger and Lukács close to one another. The example of the hammer illustrates for Heidegger that *instrumentality (Zuhandenheit)* is not the deepest form of contact of *Dasein* with its surrounding world. This *praxis, if it can be called praxis, is almost an unconscious praxis,* hence it belongs with superficial, *everyday life (Alltäglichkeit).* Nevertheless, for Heidegger, already this average everydayness contains the traces of Being. If it were otherwise, *Dasein* could never raise itself from inauthenticity. Thus the division between the ontic and the ontological is in the core of reality. Therefore, when Goldmann says, "Lukács . . . does not accept any separation between ontic and ontological, between immediate problems and philosophy" (p. 77), he wrongly attributes to Heidegger an *artificial* separation of problems and philosophy, or an artificial separation of *ontic* and *ontological.* Goldmann misinterprets equally what we called the order of priorities in the appearance of *Zuhandene* and *Vorhandene* when he claims that *Vorhandenheit* is not derived only, as Heidegger thinks, from obstacles (that *Dasein* encounters): *Vorhandenheit* constitutes a fundamental aspect of *Zuhandenheit* (p. 103).

We cannot emphasize enough the fundamental difference between these two philosophies, a difference so fundamental that it excludes comparison of the two: and we should especially eschew such language as Goldmann uses;

there is no question of deriving *Vorhandene* from *Zuhandene*. The phenomenological description does not tolerate derivation. When *Zuhandene* *appears* to be *Vorhandene,* that is, when the *instrument* appears to *Dasein* as a something being simply *there present-at-hand,* it is not the hammer that has turned into something undefinable, rather, *Dasein's* regard has turned to a new aspect of instrumentality, and this is the discovery of the *ontological* dimension of the same *ontic* reality. All this happens without a *causality* that is necessity, for if it were, everyman, every *Dasein,* would move at an equal pace towards authenticity.

It is obvious that for Lukács *Vorhandene,* that is, objects of nature not yet formed into instruments (*Zuhandene*) by man, provide the material for the initial stage of *human activity.* What Lukács means by *activity,* that is, *praxis,* which transforms both man and world, is for Heidegger *mental activity* that transforms *only* man in his effort to understand *Being.* Action originating from this *understanding* is *Dasein's* projection, that is, *Dasein's* authentic or inauthentic existence, which, moreover, can manifest itself in society, in *Dasein's* creation of its possibilities and in building its culture.

In presenting these analyses we have had no other aim than to show the profound, irreconcilable differences between Lukács and Heidegger. Since those differences cannot be brought under a common denominator, any comparison between Heidegger and Lukács proves fruitless, or, at best, must necessarily express *preferences* for the one or the other; and this is the case with Goldmann. Hence, it is not a question of *mere vocabulary* that separates Lukács from Heidegger, namely, that Heidegger wrote for a university audience while Lukács addressed Marxists belonging to unions and workers' parties, and that for this reason Lukács tried to keep to the accepted Marxist terminology as much as the topic permitted (p. 70). Goldmann attributes to this fact Lukács's adherence to the traditional vocabulary, and insists that when Lukács speaks of the separation of subject and object in traditional terms it is only to negate this separation (p. 94).

Although it was not possible in the context of our analysis to render justice to Heidegger's philosophy beyond the needs of the present discussion, his own "mise au point" concering his vocabulary should suffice to counter Goldmann's assertions and put an end to speculations that try to compare the two philosophers.

Here is Heidegger's own explanation for the "awkwardness and inelegance" of his expressions at the beginning of *Sein und Zeit,* pp. 38–39:

> With regard to the awkwardness and inelegance of expressions in the analyses to come, we may remark that it is one thing to give report in

which we tell about entities [*Seiende*], but another to grasp entities in their *Being*. For the latter task we lack not only most of the words but, above all, the "grammar" . . . and where our powers are essentially weaker, and where moreover the area of Being to be disclosed is ontologically far more difficult than that which was presented to the Greeks, the harshness of our expressions will be enhanced, and so will the minuteness of detail with which our concepts are formed.

One cannot help thinking that Goldmann's goal was to embellish Lukács's role in the shaping of Western intellectual history. Regardless of the value of those influences, if we measure their impact on emerging philosophical doctrines, Heidegger's influence by far surpasses Lukács's and I would not hesitate to give reasons for this state of affairs: the apolitical nature of Heidegger's philosophy makes for a kind of universality in its application that Lukács's politically oriented writings lack from the very beginning. But Lukács's impact could be decisive on Marxist thought if his *ontological* innovations were taken seriously. If this is ever to be the case, it will depend again on praxis, i.e., on politics, and thus Lukács may become once more the victim of his own choice.

It is the Lukács of the *Ontology* rather than the earlier Lukács who could fulfill the criterion of a comparison with Heidegger. But even here, we are forced to submit to the evidence that Lukács did not understand Heidegger, which however, does not rule out the possibility of some similarity between the two. On the other hand, Lukács's misunderstanding of Heidegger is an almost *irrefutable proof of the fundamental* difference between the two. For this reason we will analyze Lukács's interpretation of *Sein und Zeit*. After all, he is perhaps more competent than Goldmann to speak of his own relationship with a philosophy which he resisted more or less violently throughout his life. Two works stand out particularly among his writings touching on Heidegger and existential philosophy: his essay on existentialism and the historical part of the *Ontology,* which is devoted to neopositivism and existentialism. Let us now turn to these works.

Lukács and Heidegger According to Lukács

It is true that poets and philosophers are not necessarily the best interpreters of their own works. The work, although closely related to its author, enjoys an indpendence that no one can sufficiently explain; as with artistic creation, invention cannot be accounted for in terms of scientific logic. The existence of the work and its sustenance in the order of beings is part of the mysterious agency of the Spirit. It explains why a work may have an effect totally different from that intended by its "maker." This eventuality is to be maintained for every creation (artistic and intellectual); thus, Goldmann or others interpreting Lukács may have a clearer view of the influence of certain of Lukács's writings than Lukács himself.

Nevertheless, while leaving open the possibility of a message other than that intended by the author—which André Gide called *"la part de Dieu"* or *"la part du diable"*—it is important what an author thinks of another author and his work, especially if they stand far apart on the basis of their "ideologies." This is certainly the case with Heidegger and Lukács.

Lukács's encounter with Heidegger covers a long period, since they were contemporaries. There are papers, if not works, that are specifically intended to spell out in clear terms Lukács's position concerning Heidegger's innovations. The first such undertaking is found in the essay *Existentialism* (1946), in which Lukács deals in general with this novel form of philosophizing and tries to formulate its essential characteristics with reference to the two main currents in the history of philosophy—idealism and materialism. He calls Husserl's undertaking the "third way," since it wishes to avoid, by blending into one, both idealism and materialism. He explains this "third way" as an exigency imposed on bourgeois thinking by the cruel reality of the imperialistic period.[20] However, Lukács maintains the impossibility of such a conflation of philosophies and concludes that both phenomenology and existentialism are essentially variants of idealism.

Even if we set aside the embarrassing jargon of Marxist ideology and attribute it to Lukács's recent emergence from the Stalinist period (*Existentialism* was first published in 1946), this essay confirms our thesis.

Lukács views existentialism—and Heidegger's philosophy as a characteristic specimen of that new trend—as totally opposed to his own philosophy, not only in its details but in its essentials. He calls Heidegger's "fundamental ontology" an "illimited subjectivity hidden behind a false objectivity." He considers *Sein und Zeit* an exciting novel, similar to Céline's *Voyage au bout de la nuit,* a document illustrating the way of thinking and feeling of a period rather than the ontological revelation of an objective reality. It can hide its falsehood only because this way of thinking corresponds too well to the attitude of intellectuals towards an irrational, meaningless life (p. 117). Perhaps it is not an exaggeration to sum up Lukács's view on existentialism by labelling the latter "radical nihilism" (p. 115). Another salient aspect of Lukács's analysis is that he makes no distinction between the different forms of existentialism, although it is well known that Heidegger never wanted to be compared to Sartre or Jaspers.

Goldmann and his followers may object that only works up to the early

1920s can be taken as authentic in the Lukács literature, since the products of later years belong to the Stalinist period. However, there remains a disturbing fact that can hardly be reconciled with Goldmann's laudatory remarks. Is it possible that the same Lukács whose genius preceded Heidegger's innovative philosophy, and perhaps influenced this latter, could not himself understand that which he supposedly inspired in Heidegger? There is in *Existentialism* no mention of Being, subject–object identity. Only *Being-in-the-world* (*in-der-Welt-sein*) is commented on by Lukács, and his interpretation becomes an embarrassment to those who understand Heidegger and favor Lukács at the same time: "Man's life: *Mitsein* and at the same time Being-in-the world (*in-der-Welt-sein*). This being has also its own mystified and fetish-like character: "das Man," ('the one') (p. 116). Then follows the misreading of the analyses of *das Man* ("the one") and everydayness.

Nothing speaks more eloquently against Goldmann's attempt to seek similarity between Heidegger and Lukács than Lukács's total inability to situate Heidegger's work and to see the role of such notions as *Dasein, das Man,* and *In-der-Welt-sein.*

No magic can harmonize one philosophy with another if the presuppositions upon which a philosophy is based contradict this enterprise. If these remarks are not sufficiently convincing, we may multiply the proofs.

Lukács's great work the *Aesthetics* deals with an aspect of Heidegger's philosophy, and obviously with one which in *its wording* stands the closest to Marxist thought — everydayness (*Alltäglichkeit*). The *Aesthetics* was written later, in the 1950s so Lukács could have revised his earlier position on Heidegger. But this is not at all the case. The same stubborn ignorance of the Heideggerian enterprise is characteristic of this new confrontation, which Lukács calls a "comparison" of his own way of philosophizing with that of others — here, that of Heidegger — so that his own method may take shape more clearly, Lukács is aware, he says, that some would not agree when he classifies Martin Heidegger among "the romantic critics of capitalist culture" (p. 344).

Lukács finds that Heidegger's pessimistic description of *everydayness* distorts the essence of this phenomenon and does not allow the manifestation of its positive elements (pp. 344–47).

Nevertheless, Lukács understood an important aspect of the Heideggerian philosophy that Goldmann himself overlooked: the ahistorical (or suprahistorical) character of *Dasein*. He does not insist on the historicality (*Geschichtlichkeit*) of *Dasein* but he rather accuses Heidegger of withdrawing man from the *sociohistorical* context (p. 346.) In so doing, Lukács contradicts Goldmann and confirms our remarks on history and historicality in Heidegger's philosophy.

As we raise the question whether Lukács changed his position on Heidegger's philosophy in his *Ontology* twenty-five years after the publication of *Existentialism,* we really ask whether there is an evolution in his understanding of Heidegger. Our answer is a definite "no." In order to prove our point without taking our readers on a philosophical merry-go-round in the manner of Lukács, we shall single out from the historical part of the *Ontology* an example that illustrates Lukács's misinterpretation of a basic notion in *Sein und Zeit.*

This misinterpretation, like many others, stems from improper understanding of a doctrine that is far removed from Lukács's own. To begin with, Lukács is haunted by the idea of *objectivity* (as this notion is used in his *Ontology*). This means, for a thing to exist "really" is for it to be an extramental object. Lukács illustrates this at the beginning of his *Prolegomena:* "We can hunt only existing rabbits." This concept of "ontology" is the residue of old materialism, which Lukács intended to fight. However, this conception of Being is so deeply rooted in his mind that it prevents him from grasping the Heideggerian distinction between "ontic" and "ontological." Since Lukács quotes a passage from *Sein und Zeit* and also comments on it, it is easy to point out his misinterpretation.

Here is the text of *Sein und Zeit:* "So whenever an ontology takes for its theme entities whose character of Being is other than that of *Dasein,* it has its own foundation and motivation in *Dasein*'s own ontological structure, in which a pre-ontological understanding of Being is comprised as a definite characteristic. Therefore fundamental ontology, from which alone all other ontologies can take their rise, must be sought in the *existential analytic of Dasein"* (p. 13).

What is Heidegger's thesis? Since Being (*Sein*) is not an entity (*Seiende*) — not even the *highest Seiende* that medieval authors could approach in the Aristotelian tradition through its *effects,* therefore taking it for a *First Cause* (Prime Mover) — the only way to grasp Being in the Heideggerian philosophy is to have an entity (*Seiende*) that is predisposed to the understanding of Being. Thus, *Dasein,* being intermediary between *Sein* (Being) and *Seiende* (entities), becomes the starting point both towards the understanding of the meaning of Being and also the understanding of entities in the world.

Lukács interprets the Heideggerian text "in plain language" and says that Heidegger's ontology takes only man and his social relations into consideration. But even here, Heidegger rejects an ontology of social being; furthermore, in his ontology all the evident ontological problems of nature disappear as irrelevant. Lukács accuses Heidegger of polemicizing emphatically against all ontologies that claim to find anything primary in nature. Of course, Lukács can only misquote Heidegger on being-in-the-world (*in-der-Welt-sein*) and the problem of nature. It is obvious that when a philosopher tries to impose on another, as Lukács attempts to do with Heidegger, his notion of the *world (Welt)*, he cannot follow the argument of his opponent. Should we remind Lukács that for Heidegger "to give a phenomenological (ontologic) description of the *world* will mean to exhibit the Being of those entities which are present-at-hand with the world, and to fix it in concepts which are categorial"? Then, what is the *world* for Heidegger? "Is it possible that ultimately we cannot address ourselves to 'the world' as determining the nature of the entity we have mentioned? Yet we call this entity one which is "within-the-world." Is 'world' perhaps a characteristic of *Dasein*'s Being?"[21]

Is it not a pity to see that Lukács has to fall back into his old habit of characterizing Heidegger as a bourgeois philosopher? "All categories that Heidegger means to establish through his phenomenological–ontological research of *Dasein* are nothing but highly abstract categories; they are the direct manifestations of modern capitalistic-alienated and manipulated life, freely translated by Heidegger into an original picturesque language."[22]

Some Problems of Terminology

The *Ontology* speaks of *what is.* But in all discourse we use language to express what we mean; hence terminological rigor is the first requirement in all ontological speculations. We maintained that the usefulness of ontology consisted exactly in the clarification of matters that make agreement and disagreement possible and dialogue fruitful.

However, as we have often seen in the chapter on Goldmann, Lukács, and Heidegger, similarities among doctrines were based on misunderstanding of terms; and Goldmann and Lukács were equally liable to such offences.

In order to help to understand the problem under dicussion — without any intention to decide the question — we wish to stress the meaning of a few terms that can be particularly misleading.

First, the opinion of Heidegger on Marxism in the *Letter on Humanism.* This opinion concerns Marxism as a philosophy that, among other things, speaks of man and beings. In this little book, which was written especially to redress certain misinterpretations of his major work, *Sein und Zeit,* Heidegger likens Marxism to metaphysics and other types of humanism that consider the humanity of *homo humanus* from the viewpoint of a fixed intepretation of nature, history, world, and foundation of the world; that is, of bieng in its totality ("auf dem Hinblick auf eine schon feststehende Auslegung der Natur, der Geschichte, der Welt, des Weltgrundes, das heisst des Seienden im Ganzen").[23]

What Heidegger calls *metaphysics* "in the traditional meaning of the term" is a science of *beings* (*Seiende*) and not the science of *Being* (*Sein*), which is the main concern of his own ontology. One should not overlook the distinction between speculations on the *ontic* and the *ontological* level.

This will explain that, although Heidegger does not give Marxism as an example to illustrate metaphysical thinking, his remarks apply to it, as they apply to other metaphysical thinking of humanism, including Christianity. "Metaphysics (hence Marxism as metaphysics) thinks man beginning with his animality and therefore it does not think the direction of his humanity." Man's humanity unfolds in his existence and one may say, by means of language. This is how language becomes the house of Being (*die Sprache ist das Haus des Seins*). Man dwells in language. There is no way to claim that the kind of existence ascribed to man by Heidegger and which is called by him the essence of man could be compared to any other definition of man as an essence, including that of Marx: "(Man) is a being for himself, and therefore a species being."[24]

We had no other aim in quoting Heidegger's own clarification of the essential notions of *Sein und Zeit* than to confirm the difference between Lukács and Heidegger with reference to *Dasein* and man, Being and Totality.

We can only deplore hasty comparisons between Heidegger and Lukács that are based more on superficial similarity than on essential, fundamental agreement on basics in the two doctrines. Goldmann, however, is not the only one to commit this error. There is, if not a general tendency, at least a kind of consensus among Western Marxist authors who wish to enhance Lukács's reputation (even at the risk of making him an outcast in the Eastern Marxist camp,) to liken him to Heidegger, who is, without any doubt, the most prestigious philosopher of modern times.

Andrew Feenberg, in his article "Reification and Antimonies of Socialist Thought" puts forth a suggestion that in *The Theory of the Novel* Lukács's position was not unlike that of the later Heidegger in certain respect, and he cites as an example of this similarity the notion of totality.[25]

Feenberg speaks of the unity of Lukács's work using Frederik Jameson's article, *"The Case for Georg Lukács."*[26]

Already, in *The Theory of the Novel*, Feenberg claims, Lukács employed the idea of totality: "As applied to Greece, the totality is the harmonious union of essence and life, man and world. When essence and form can be discovered in things just as they are, then there is totality."[27]

However, this idea of totality, Feenberg admits, is *ambiguous*. This can be said about all philosophical notions employed by Marxist philosophers, and it applies to Feenberg's clarification also. "Totality," as applied to Greece, says Feenberg, "is the *harmonious* union of essence and life," hence *totality is harmony.* Then, how to conceive *harmony?* Here Feenberg again interprets Lukács and writes: "When *essence* and *form* can be discovered in *things just as they are,* when life offers an objective meaning in which men discover themselves just as they are, then there is totality."[28]

If Feenberg relies on accepted philosophical usage of such terms as *essence, form, things as they are,* or *objective meaning,* his sentence is unintelligible. If he uses those terms metaphorically, his own interpretation of Lukács needs an interpretation. In this sense, the unity of Lukács's work is explained *metaphorically* rather than *philosophically.* The term "totality" is not an ontological concept as it is in the *Ontology,* but a cultural notion: one reconciles oneself with nature or the world and through one's art projects harmony into one's life.

Noting this distinction between Heidegger and Lukács is only a warning against further serious misreadings of Heidegger. One should bear in mind equally the difference in the usage of the term "ontology," not only by the later Lukács and Heidegger but also by Heidegger and traditional ontology (metaphysics). Only the ignorance of such essential differences could have made Feenberg say that "Heidegger interprets a few lines of Hölderlin from precisely the point of view of a millenial nihilism"[29] which is analysed by Lukács in his *The Theory of the Novel.*

It is customary to speak about Heidegger's nihilism. Indeed, Heidegger writes in his *What Is Metaphysics?* that *"Das Nicht offenbart das Sein"* ("Nothingness reveals Being"). But is it not time for all to realize that Heidegger's approach to Being (*Sein*) has nothing in common with nihilism, likewise his interpretatin of Hölderlin's poem?[30]

However, what is more appalling than such misreadings of Heidegger is the intention of the author to draw from ill-conceived premises a value judgment in favor of Lukács, saying that he represents a still deeper level of abandonment before the " 'failure of God' " than Heidegger, "since the recognition of the failure of the old God in irony refuses to become itself a new sort of religion."[31]

Since our purpose here is not to write an apology for Heidegger's way of dealing with problems related to ontology, we point only to the issue in question, namely, Lukács's relationship with Heidegger.

We may conclude that the misreadings of commentators do not contribute to the better understanding of the two philosophies.

Chapter 6   INSTEAD OF A CONCLUSION: THE
SHAPING OF THE NOTION OF PERSON
IN LUKÁCS'S *ONTOLOGY*

An ontology, by definition, has no conclusion; it has implications that make its application possible. Once the elaboration of its principles is completed, the work is over. Next comes the application of those principles to the concrete.

Reflections upon an ontology must follow the same line. A conclusion would only be the recapitulation of the main points of a doctrine, which we consider here unnecessary repetition.

It is true that we could also write a prophetic message on what we consider to be the future of Lukács's *Ontology* and its impact on Marxist thinking; but again, such a venture goes against the nature of ontology. Ontology speaks about *what is* and not about what will effectively happen, especially when human freedom is involved in the shaping of a future. The safest way to close these reflections is to state what has happened so far. As to the impact of the *Ontology,* we must say that it has had none. It seems to be enshrined in its own prison, its bulk and its style, which make it inaccessible to readers who look for a clear exposition of a doctrine. Indeed, it is plagued with tortuous digressions and sometimes contradictions. Even its important innovations are hidden under traditional quotations from classical Marxist writings, which supply material for those who do not want to see fundamental changes introduced into Marxist thinking. They are able to find in it the confirmation of their traditional views and on this ground negate the novelty of Lukács's *Ontology*.

Furthermore, what affects the *Ontology* most is the disappearance of the grand old man of Marxism, its author whose personality — while he was alive was in itself of interest to Marxist and non-Marxist alike.

In sum, the *Ontology,* because of its length and constant reference to the classic Marxist literature, covers up and obscures the important changes it proposes; in some cases, perhaps, inadvertently. The whole enterprise is presented in such a way that revised Marxism seems already contained in Marx, whom Lukács names at the beginning as the one who laid down the foundation of a Marxist ontology.

104

Could it be that Lukács himself did not realize that instead of giving a firm ontological basis for Marxism he had shaken it to its very foundation by showing the insufficiency of its first principle, matter? From that moment on, the innovations followed the law of implications of ontological principles: consciousness, freedom, necessity, evolution; then, on the epistemological level, *Widerspiegelung* (reflection) had to undergo the required changes.

As we mentioned, ontology can only speak about *what is* and not about what will happen, except in a theoretical way, and this requires the employment of the law of implication. This being so, we can *theorize* only about the influence of Lukács's work on future Marxist thought, and we can say that it will be read and discussed when Marx's eleventh thesis on Feuerbach is inverted, to wit, before changing the world, we must understand it; understanding means interpretation; in other terms: praxis must seek its theoretical foundation. But such a change would transform Marxist ideology into Marxist philosophy, and we do not know whether Lukács wanted to go so far.

In order to remain faithful to our own method, we would not wish to speculate any further on the future of the *Ontology*. Instead, we will give another direction to our reflections, once more in agreement with the ontological method. In order to test Lukács's ontological system, we shall propose its application to an issue discussed also in another system, or even borrowed from another system, and show, in this way, the solutions proposed by the respective systems.

This exercise, however, will be profitable only if we are able to avoid the ideological bias whose aim would be the affirmation of the superiority of one system over another. On the other hand, if we fear to run the risk of such an enterprise, we shall remain forever entangled in a terminology that recoils on itself and contributes only to the perpetuation of phraseologies that finish by becoming meaningless, even to those who have invented them. Is it not through application that terms are truly clarified and understood? Then, we shall propose one example, borrowed form an "ideology" that is at the antipode of Marxism, the notion of person that could properly introduce us into the most controversial issue of Marxism. Already the title of Lukács's work — *The Ontology of Social Being* — indicates that Marxism gives another interpretation of social phenomena than did traditional ontology, which based its theory on the anthropological definition of man, stressing his aboriginal uniqueness, not only as being in creation, but also as an individual, as opposed to man in society.

It is well known that Marxist thinkers do not stress man's uniqueness at the expense of sociability, because even if they wanted to do so they would be prevented by their own ontological principle — matter — which allows the conception of man only as an epiphenomenon, i.e., as determined by matter. Thus, to affirm the uniqueness of man and his "species being" (as does Marx) is only a sentimental stance that is lacking ontological foundation.

Social reality taught Lukács the unavoidable truth, that Marxism in its old form had to be surpassed, and that the first leg of this journey was the *theoretical* freeing of man from the bondage of matter, since his uniqueness was already *de facto* recognized.

Labor as a means towards the self-realization of man and the affirmation of his unique ontological status, i.e., the affirmation that human consciousness was *not an epiphenomenon,* became an ontological necessity. But, one may ask: where does the emancipation of man end? To be free (i.e., to have a consciousness not determined by matter) implies the difficult question: *how free*? In other words, in setting as our aim the elaboration of an ontology — or, as we have said, applying the term strictly to Lukács's undertaking: a *theory of praxis* — we are bound to answer even those questions that originally we had not intended to raise. Moreover, our answer has to contain almost the same elements as in a philosophy, where we find that notion developed. Does it mean that the laws of ontology are necessary once they are applied — intentionally or only accidentally — to a concrete example, in our case, to the notion of person? The only choice one has is to leave the question unanswered. The shaping of the notion of person in Lukács's doctrine is a similar issue; hence, our reflections on this problem could adequately exemplify the ontological approach and its built-in rigor.

We shall, then, use the notion of person to test the internal consistency of Lukács's doctrine relative to man and to observe through the shifting emphasis on ontological principles the compulsion to follow out all the implications of those principles when applied to social and individual life. When discussing the notion of person in Lukács's *Ontology,* we extend the term "ontology" far beyond his latest work, and we also include what can be considered "ontological" in his earlier work. We shall witness in the shaping of the notion of person a curious phenomenon: not only did Lukács borrow even in his earlier period elements form Christian ontology, but, besides, we witness the leveling off of differences between doctrines that are far apart when viewed from their starting points. This fact speaks in favor of the usefulness of ontology in general: (1) ontology can be either the ground for a dialogue between different "ideologies" or (2) for the stating of their ultimate distinction.

The Notion of Person: A Christian Notion

Although the term "person" is readily understood by all, its meaning is more difficult to grasp when we look back on its historical development.

However, the reflections that follow have a purpose other than the historical reconstruction of the meaning of *person*. Therefore, I only note for clarity's sake that it is an accepted opinion among philosophers that the notion of *person* emerged in late antiquity and that it originates in the speculations of Christian theologians and philosophers on the dual nature of Christ (the incarnation) and the mystery that surrounds the Trinity.[1] As the context already indicates, the notion of *person* is meant to overcome the paradox of such irreconcilable opposites as body and soul, finite and infinite, necessity and freedom. Since the difficulty lies in the coexistence of these opposites in the *concrete;* a person cannot be an abstraction such as an essence or a universal; not even an individual specimen of a class, such as a man. The person is a unique individual whose spiritual nature is dependent on a being that is Spirit itself, such as God, and who is also a Person. This means that if God is a person, He cannot be an abstraction, i.e., an essence or the idealization of some qualities (Beauty, Goodness, Perfection, etc.).

By saying that the notion of *person* is a Christian notion I do not mean that one would not find elsewhere in other religious or cultural traditions the necessary requirements for being a person. I only stress the fact that Christian philosophers and theologians were the first to reflect upon this problem which later became a philosophical (esp. a moral) issue. Now, it is well known that religion in general and Christianity in particular were considered by classical Marxism the leading ideology—due to their social and historical role—that Marxism had to combat.

In the *Philosophisches Wörterbuch* published in Leipzig and which reflects the Marxist-Leninist approach to philosophical problems, *Person* is not listed, only *Persönlichkeit*. The definition corresponding to what we call, according to Western tradition *person* is the following: "the idealization and absolutization of man's inner life, the "intimate sphere" of a person [*person*], the reference to a spiritual conception of the self which is exempt from struggle and social progress; it is a reference to the withdrawal into the "inner self" characterized by such a conception."[2] The later history of Marxism, especially the intention of Lukács to continue Marx, revealed the same paradox in the heart of Marxist philosophy: the moral agent has to be a person, with all the charcteristics attributed to that notion by Christian philosophers, with the exception of the person's dependence on God. As we have seen in the chapter on *Terrorism and the Notion of Freedom* Lukács had already attempted at the beginning of his career as Marxist philosopher, to overcome this paradox. This indicates that even a philosophy that has not issued from Christin tradition, such as Marxism, but whose presuppositions attempt to explain social phenomena and sociopolitical transformations, necessarily evolves towards at least an implicit notion of person. These remarks are not to be interpreted as the denial of such notions as *human being, individual,* or *person* in the context of Marxist ideological writings. My intention is to suggest only that specific terms of our language may increase or decrease in significance when they pass from one doctrine to another. Hence, the mere appearance of a term is no guarantee of its traditional content.

In this sense, we may disregard the fact that the history of person begins in Christian tradition, because we affirm that to be a person is more than an accidental feature of being a man.

Of course, the term *accidental* calls for its opposite, the *essential,* and suggests that to be a man is to be a person. If essences are ultimate possibilities — and what else could they be — the affirmation that all men are potentially persons should perhaps replace the term "man." This would suggest that *some individuals* are *only men,* which would certainly not help to clarify the issue. It is, therefore, advisable to remain with the first formulation and to say that to be a person is more than an accidental feature of being a man, meaning that the humanity of man reaches its climax in being a person, which corresponds to Boethius's definition, namely, "the individual substance of a rational nature." Out of this definition flow the implications of rationality and individuality, which recall the specific form of exercising our freedom.

In this sense, although we associate the history of *person* with Christian tradition, such a notion may arise at least as a problem in any doctrine, hence in Marxism also.

The history of Marxism shows, and the itinerary of Lukács supplies the example, that philosophical problems, including the problem of person, necessarily arise in *praxis* as soon as *praxis* seeks its justifiction. In the concrete, this will be the case when the general notion of *praxis* is translated into *tactics* through particular acts to realize the desired change. Thus tactics supercedes the old laws of ethics that have been turned into interpretation of the world by Marx's eleventh thesis. Indeed, ethical laws and precepts either are derived form interpretations of the world, or they imply an interpretation of the world. In Marxian terms, ethics becomes "an apologia for the existing order of things or at least the proof of their immutability." Hence tactics, or the justification of tactics, should also become an interpretation of the world: in Marxian terms, an ideology, if we qualify this undertaking as an activity that justifies the establishment of a new order.

Calling an ethics "ideology" is equivalent with its devaluation, and thus with the freeing of individuals from the obligation to abide by its commandments. Whereas it is easy to change an interpretation regulating manipulation of goods or even some kind of interrelationship between individuals and society, when faced with the law that governs murder, e.g., as in a case of an act of terrorism required by tactics, the philosophy of praxis can no longer qualify this part of ethics as interpretation or self-justification, i.e., ideology. It seems as if, beyond the metaphysical foundation of moral laws, or the pragmatic and behaviorist interpretations of human conduct, some laws belong to an unwritten code of ethics whose foundation is so deeply rooted in humanity that searching for it is the same as searching for the origin of mankind. This is the problem that faces George Lukács in his early work *Tactics and Ethics*. Since interpretation of human actions must touch off an interpretation of "human being" and must spell out explicitly the characteristics that underlie all moral acts, we find in this writing the first theoretical approach to the question of what we can call a notion of person that transcends "ideologies."

The relationship the murderer has with the act in the specific context of an act of terrorism is contained in the following presupposition: freedom and obligation are placed under the law of the *collective reason of history*. The specific obligation of the terrorist exemplifies here the tension that sets into motion the dialectic of the general and the individual, a dialectic which is the primary, even if it is not the sufficient, condition of becoming a person. Hence, for the time being, we may accept that this dialectic is capable of producing an individual as opposed to a collective being, considering that an individual has to realize the highest possible degree of freedom in a system of collective values that are binding for him. It is worth noting that Lukács sets the exigency very high, and he even heightens the conflict by confronting the "general" with an "individual" in the category of exceptions, namely, the terrorist. His solution of the conflict brings out the intention of Lukács, or, if we wish, *das Ungedachte* of Lukács: the communist terrorist is the counterpart of the Christian saint. If Lukács's interpretation of the conflict between the obligation dictated by the collective reason of history and the individual's conscious submission to the reason that contravenes the laws of ethics is right, the terrorist becomes a sort of hero of faith, an exceptional individual, who sacrifices his purity for a value of a higher order, that of collectivity.

We meet here with the first stumbling block on the road to becoming a *person*. A person, in the ordinary sense of the term, namely in the legal sense, is someone who has the competence to bear responsibility and against whom charges can be laid in accordance with the criteria. In the case of the terrorist, the tribunal is the collective reason of history, whose commandments are translated by the terrorist into appropriate or inappropriate acts judged by the success or failure of the undertaking. In this context, terrorists become *instruments* in the hands of history, and for the sake of the *collectivity* their acts produce, instead of the sharpening of the consciousness of individuality, self-effacement in favor of the collectivity. This self-effacement may, indeed, be the mark of authentic self-sacrifice, as is the case for the saint, and the highest realization of individuality in its conscious relationship with the absolute. Lukács understood this very well. But what he did not understand was the difference between the two types of relationships: (1) the terrorist is related *impersonally* to an entity considered absolutely *impersonal,* the collective reason of history; his success and failure is measured in *outward* acts, judged moral or immoral by the dialectic of history; (2) the knight of faith is related *personally* to an absolute that is also a *person;* their relationship is an *inwardness* expressed by the tension between the *finite* and the *infinite* and measured by the *intention* that lifts up the finite to the infinite; the outward manifestation of success and failure is only accidental to the accomplishment of the act; the self-effacement is a self-accomplishment or fulfillment of the self in its highest form of consciousness; therefore, there is no tribunal other than the self that experiences an inner reward, a reward by definition *spiritual* and incommunicable.

Whether this early writing, *Tactics and Ethics,* truly reflects Lukács's thinking can be tested against his well-known work, *History and Class Consciousness.* Speaking about class consciousness in the essay bearing the same title, Lukács quotes Marx in exergue: "The question is not what goal is *envisaged* for the time being by this or that member of the proletariat, or even by the proletariat as a whole. The question is *what is the proletariat* and what course of action will it be forced historically to take in conformity with its own *nature.*"[3]

This quotation underlies our analysis of *Tactics and Ethics,* and what follows will confirm that, although Lukács attempted in his paper a reconciliation of the individual with the class or society taking on an intermediary — history — he failed to produce a satisfactory answer to the problem by depriving the terrorist of the inward enjoyment of his sacrifice.

The essay on *Class Consciousness* offers numerous examples that support our interpretation. The text quoted from Engels argues on the same line as Marx, and Lukács draws the conclusion: "The essence of scientific Marxism consists, then, in the realization that the real motor forces of history are independent of man's (psychological) consciousness of them."[4]

There is sacrifice only in the conscious acceptance of a chosen lot; to be a martyr is something other than to be a victim because the precondition of sacrifice is freedom of choice and teleological positioning (*teleologische Setzung*). Lukács's terrorist is both victim and martyr, since the Marxist thesis maintains that man can have little or no effect on the fundamental motive of history: conformity to laws, and an objectivity that is independent of human will and in particular the wills of individual man.[5]

Now, if for one to fulfill one's duty towards one's fellows is to follow the commandments of history, one's personal relationship with others might be reduced to the mere acknowledgement of their existence. The other consequence of this thesis is the impossiblity for individuals to have any influence on the unfolding of forces in history. Under such circumstances, "the spirit of the people" or "great men" can only be described pragmatically, but cannot be understood rationally, i.e., ontologically. One may submit them only as a sort of work of art, to an "aesthetic organization." Or, one must grasp them, as in the philosophy of history of the Kantians, as material for the realization of an atemporal, suprahistoric, and ethical principle, which, according to Lukács, has no meaning in itself. It is therefore evident that in spite of relations between men, what constitutes history is not the relation "between one individual and another, but between worker and capitalist . . ."[6]

Of course, what follows seems to tone down this statement, because Lukács adds that people have in such relationships only the consciousness of essential determinations belonging to their existence. I raise doubts about the intensity of such relationships as compared to the relationship of person to person, without mentioning the distortion that necessarily occurs as soon as I envisage my neighbor as a "general," a "universal," a "worker," or a "capitalist," instead of "this" person or "that" person. One should not forget the dangers ethics faces in such *impersonal* relationships.

We may conclude with Lukács that "the historically significant actions of the class as a whole are determined, in the last resort by this (class) consciousness and not by the thought of the individual."[7] Since the goal is to bring about the desired change, the duty of an individual is to be attentive to history in order to objectify the right consciousness of a situation which implies clearly the limitations imposed by this theory on the notion of person, even if one does not go as far as to state that the highest achievement required of a person is to become an *anti-person*.

When taken in its historical context, Lukács's writing can be classified as belonging to the period of revolutionary praxis. This interpretation may take away the edge of collectivism as a permanent form of human existence. In sum, in the early writings of Lukács the value of the self depends on the determination it receives form society, history, or the *class*. Here, the self as consciousness should become class consciousness in order not to be false consciousness.

However, is there not a difference between being class conscious and being ethical? In other terms, one may build a revolution on a class, but not an everyday moral life. Lukács intended to present the terrorist as an exception to the rules of ethics, hence an exceptional man, whose acts, if historically correct, justify the teleological suspension of ethics—then, instead of being an ordinary murderer, the terrorist would fall into the category of tragic hero. But what about an "ordinary" murder and other acts that interfere—to some degree—with the life of others, once the desired social change is brought about? It is just common sense that exceptions cannot be turned into the general rule of ethics. Furthermore, a class can be conscious of its historical role, and thus it is conceivable that workers are opposed to capitalists. But can a class, whether the working class or the bourgeoisie, be in itself ethical? An ethics implies the existence of moral persons. Then who is a moral person or what should be an ethics for Marxism? Since ethics spells out the criterion of values, and here values must include also those which individuals as such realize in their lives, should we not rehabilitate individual differences and great men, i.e., exceptional individuals, who have been sacrificed by Lukács to the collective reason of history?

Once communism is established, could the revolutionary praxis be maintained? Lukács answered this question forty years later when he undertook the elaboration of an ethics for Marxism. It is worth noting that Lukács continued his reflection where he left off, with the relationship of individuals to society.

At this point, the reflections of Lukács make a full circle, supporting our thesis that even philosophies that place society or class above the individual evolve necessarily towards the notion of person as an inevitable *ontological* necessity. We find in this development the justification of the claim that the person is the highest in the hierarchy of forms that the "essence" of humankind can take during the course of its "existential" embodiment.

This new conception of the role and value of individuals and great men came to light already in the Vienna paper ("The ontological foundation of human thinking and action"). In this paper, Lukács tried to overcome a dilemma, namely, that of the determinism of social context—history—and the freedom of individuals; he endeavors to save individual differences, that is, the qualitative, the exceptional. But his undertaking was doomed to fail, as we have seen, because of his ontological presupposition: the material principle.[8]

Our analysis of the Vienna paper has shown that the ontological presuppositions Lukács accepted unexamined kept him entangled in their inevitable ontological implications; thus, Lukács failed to secure the freedom and independence necessary for a "social being" to become a person. Of course, as long as man is considered an epiphenomenon and consciousness a late product of matter, it will be vain to attempt to save individual differences, and along with them the notion of person.

However, in the *Ontology of Social Being* Lukács introduces major revisions that affect his fundamental presuppositions in the interpretation of consciousness. Only animal consciousness is an epiphenomenon, a product of nature, determined by matter. Lukács no longer considers human consciousness to be an epiphenomenon. This shift in his position is meant to explain human freedom that manifests itself in labor and in what Lukács calls "*teleologische Setzungen*" ("teleological positioning" or "purposive acts"). Is it permissible to speculate that this change was meant to save man's creativity and what we called in the Vienna paper individual differences and their underlying principle, a consciousness capable of surpassing even nature's inventiveness?

As a result of this change of principle, the famous theory of *Widerspiegelung* must also go. It is on this ground that Lukács's disciples point out the conflict between the solution proposed in *History and Class Consciousness* and in the *Ontology*. Would it be an exaggeration to claim that the ground is now cleared for the emergence of "person," even if it remains only a possibility, since Lukács's death put an end to its further unfoldings? We advance this thesis as the *Ungedachte* of Lukács.

The final evidence we are able to produce in favor of this thesis is the interview Lukács gave to the editor of *Vigilia* shortly before his death.[9] Here, Lukács compares his commitment to that of a Jeanne d'Arc or Christian martyrs who secured immortality in the memory of people through their unwavering fidelity to their commitment. In his own commitment, his "Marxist scientism" turns into a kind of *faith,* and thus becomes an internal relation with an ideal, even if this ideal is, in his case, a historical reality—the dictatorship of the proletariat.

What is the turning point in the shaping of the notion of "person" in Lukács's *Ontology?* It is, in short, the interiorization of our relation with a reality that is considered "above" the individual and the abandonment of external success or failure as the criterion of value.

To accomplish this interiorization, man has to have both *capability* and *choice.* The old conception of consciousness as epiphenomenon offered only limited capability, and, theoretically, no choice. Lukács's decision *to widen the gap between matter and consciousness* (or matter and intellect) moves towards an anthropological definition of man which Max Scheler considered as the condition *sine qua non* of becoming a person. As is shown throughout Scheler's famous book—*Formalism in Ethics and Non-Formal Ethics of Values*—even the Kantian solution, which postulates freedom and calls man an end in itself, falls short of this requirement because the person has to be the bearer of values; then values, in Scheler's ethics, are nonformal, material values; that is they need a *person,* and not only a consciousness, to experience them.[10]

Moreover, individual differences presuppose also personal identity, and personal identity is unthinkable without a person, i.e., without an anthropological definition of man. We only mention in passing that Hartmann's suggestion—the distinction between ontological and epistemological—holds true in the case of personal identity as well. Therefore, the speculations on personal identity now so common in empiricist circles also fall short of the criterion of being a person, because they remain on the epistemological level.

With "faith," a new element surfaces in Lukács's philosophy. Faith in one's vocation enables the individual to bear the consequences of a self-imposed commitment, especially if this commitment endangers one's life. At the same time, faith is always the individualization, hence the interiorization, of a decision. Thus sacrifice, even if it be tactically useless, transends the sphere of necessity, and moves towards the sphere of freedom; that is, ethics.

Although Lukács can never resist the temptation to insinuate that religion is a form of alienation, he borrows his values from it. I have listed two examples: the terrorist as saint, and fidelity to commitment as a form of immortality in the memory of people. They illustrate how ethics becomes in every philosophy a ladder leading towards spiritual values. Hence one who acts morally is on the way to becoming a person—a bridge between the finite and the infinite.

This last example shows that although Lukács lost his fight for the internal consistency of his doctrine, his intention remains even as a failure, a great moral victory, and secures the internal consistency of his life; thus it points towards the criterion of *intellectual tactics*—which is *intellectual honesty*. Intellectual honesty, on the other hand, implies the laying bare of one's ontological presuppositions and the examination of their implictions. This makes the consequences of their application foreseeable and justifies the labelling of this intellectual exercise the proper understanding of an autocriticism.

Notes

Chapter 1

1. Cf. George Novack, *Georg Lukács as a Marxist Philosopher,* in George Novack, *Polemics in Marxist Philosophy* (New York: Monad Press, 1978), pp. 117–34. Page citations in the text are to this edition.
2. Béla Hegyi, *A dialógus sodrában* (Budapest: Magvetö, 1978), pp. 28-49; here published in English translation for the first time, as Appendix I, pp.
3. Found in the papers left by Prof. M. Wattnick to Prof. David Spitz who taught at the Graduate Center of the City University of New York. Prof. Spitz intended to donate these papers to the Archives of the University Library. He died in February 1980.
4. *Tactics and Ethics* was published for the first time in Hungarian during the Communist Revolution of 1919 in a journal of the same title. Later, Lukács included this article in a selection of his works in Hungarian, entitled *Utam Marxhoz* (*"My Road to Marx"*). In the preface to this selection dated 1969, Lukács speaks of a crisis in his life that found its solution in his article *Taktika és etika* and in his joining the communist party. The German text of *Tactics and Ethics* is printed in the second volume of Lukács's *Complete Works,* published by Luchterhand, 1968, pp. 45-54. An English translation of the German text has been published by Harper Torchbooks, 1975, under the title *Tactics and Ethics:* Political Essays, 1919-1929. It was translated by Michael McColgan and edited with an introduction by Rodney Livingstone, pp. 3-11.
5. Hegyi, *Dialógus:* see Appendix I.
6. New York: Monad Press, 1978.
7. Georg Lukács, *Geschichte und Klassenbewusstsein* (Berlin and Neuwied: Hermann Luchterhand Verlag, 1968); *Histoire et conscience de classe,* trans. K. Axelos and J. Bois (Paris: Les Editions de Minuit, 1960): *History and Class Consciousness,* trans. Rodney Livingstone (London: Merlin Press, 1971).
8. Roger Garaudy, *Marxism in the Twentieth Century,* trans. René Hague (London: Collins, 1970).
9. Louis Althusser, *For Marx,* trans. Ben Brewster (New York: Random House, 1969).
9A. Louis Althusser and Etienne Balibar, *Lire le Capital I* (Paris: Maspero, 1968), p. 6: " . . . la définition (donnée dans *Pour Marx* et reprise dans la Préface à *Lire le Capital*) de la philosophie comme *théorie de la pratique théorique* est unilatérale et donc inexacte. En l'occurence, il ne s'agit pas d'une simple équivoque de terminologie, mais d'une erreur dans la conception même."
10. Georg Klaus and Manfred Buhr, eds., *Philosophisches Wörterbuch,* 2 vols. (Leipzig: VEB Bibliographisches Institut, 1970), vol. 2:865-73.
11. George Lukács, *Utam Marxhoz* (*"My Road to Marx"*), 2 vols. (Budapest: Magvetó, 1971).
12. *Zur Ontologie des gesellschaftlichen Seins,* Part I, *"Die gegenwärtige Problemlage"*, intro-

115

duction, p. 2. (My translation.) This is a yet unpublished part of the *Ontology* in the German original. Luchterhand published the following chapters: *"Hegels echte und falsche Ontologie"*; *"Die ontologischen Grundprinzipien von Marx"*; *"Die Arbeit"*. The rest of the work is available only in manuscript (found in the "Lukács Archives" in Budapest; the call number of the Ontology is: LAK/99-185): *"Neo-Positivismus und Existentialismus"*; *"Nikolai Hartmanns Vorstoss zu einer echten Ontologie"*; *"Die Reproduktion"*; *"Das Ideelle und die Ideologie"*; *"Die Entfremdung"*; and *"Die Prolegomena"*, which was written last. I thank the "Lukács Archives" of Budapest for allowing me to have a copy of Lukács's typed manuscript. The Archive is set up in Lukács's old apartment; the address is: Lukács Archivum, Budapest, V., Belgrád rakpart 2.

13. Ibid., p. 4. (My translation.)
14. Could we say that Lukács tried to bridge the gap by using Nikolai Hartmann's descriptive, i.e. presuppositionless ontology? The shortcomings of Lukács's method become visible later in our analysis of his ontological principles.
15. Hegyi, *Dialógus,* p. 33; Appendix I. p.
16. Lukács, *Utam Marxhoz,* vol. I, pp. 22-23. (My translation.)
17. Ibid., p. 23. (My translation.)
18. Ibid., p. 22. (My translation.)
19. Novack, *Polemics,* pp. 117 – 34. Cf. Hegyi, *Dialógus;* see Appendix I.
20. Lucien Goldmann, *Lukács et Heidegger* (Paris: Denoël-Gonthier, 1973).
21. Pp. 24-25. (My translation.)
22. Hegyi, *Dialógus,* pp. 35-36; Appendix I. pp.
23. Ibid., pp. 34-35; Appendix I, pp.

Chapter 2

1. Béla Hegyi, *A dialógus sodrában* (Budapest: Magvető, 1978), p. 33; here published in English translation for the first time, as Appendix I, pp.
2. Ibid., p. 48; Appendix I, pp.
3. Cf. George Novack, *"Georg Lukács as a Marxist Philosopher"*, in George Novack, *Polemics in Marxist Philosophy* (New York: Monad Press, 1978). pp. 117-134. Novack refers to Lukács 's role in the Hungarian Communist Revolution of 1919.
4. Georg Lukács, *Die ontologischen Grundlagen des menschlichen Denkens und Handelns,* in Lukács, *Utam Marxhoz ("My Road to Marx"),* 2 vols. (Budapest: Magvetö, 1971), 2: 542-64 (in Hungarian); here published in English translation for the first time, as Appendix II, pp.

Chapter 3

1. Béla Hegyi, *A dialógus sodrában* (Budapest: Magvetö, 1978), p. 30; here published in English translation for the first time, as Appendix I, pp. 124-34.
2. George Lukács, *Tactics and Ethics,* trans. Michael McColgan (New York: Harper and Row,

1975), p.11.
3. " . . . we have to be cautioned that without proper analysis of the economic process, all evaluation is only popular wisdom. I see in the tacticism, which is a sort of opportunism, the obstacle to the revival of theoretical work. Instead of applying intelligence to the improvement and criticism of practice, we subjugate it to momentary needs." Hegyi, *Dialógus*, p. 34; Appendix I, p. 127.
4. Hegyi, *Dialógus, p. 33; Appendix I, p. 127.*

Chapter 4

1. Robert V. Daniels, *The Nature of Communism* (New York: Vintage Books, 1964), p. 17: An ideology, according to Marx, is a system of beliefs — including legal, philosophical, religious, and other ideas — generated in a given society and serving to justify the status quo and the interest of the ruling class. "The ideas of the ruling class," wrote Marx and Engels in 1864, "are, in every age, the ruling ideas . . . The dominant ideas are nothing more than the ideal expression of the dominant material relationship . . . which make one class the ruling one."
2. V.V. Mshveniredza, *"Philosophy and Ideology",* in *Proceedings of the Fourteenth International Congress of Philosophy* (Vienna, 1968), I: 412.
3. Ibid., p. 413.
4. *Herders Kleines Philosophisches Wörterbuch,* eds. Max Müller and Alois Halder (Freiburg im Bresgau: Verlag Herder, 11. ed., 1969), p. 8.
5. Cf. Paul Ricoeur, *"Science et idéologie,"* *Revue philosophique de Louvain* 72 (1974): 365. "Abstract: following on the work of the Frankfurt School and that of Althusser in France, the theories of social sciences lay claim to exorcise ideologies". Cf. also Hans-Georg Gadamer's debate with Jürgen Habermas on Hermeneutic and Ideology.
6. Georg Lukács, *Die ontologischen Grundlagen des menschlichen Denkens und Handelns* was first published in *Ad lectores* 8 (Neuwied-Berlin: Luchterhand Verlag, 1969), pp. 148–64. Since it was a paper prepared for the Fourteenth International Congress of Philosophy, held in Vienna in 1968, I refer to it throughout the text as the "Vienna paper" (VP). Page references in the text are to this edition. (Translations are mine.) The Vienna paper is here published in English translation for the first time as Appendix II, pp. 135-49.
7. Hans-Georg Gadamer, *Kleine Schriften,* 3 vols. (Tübingen: Mohr, 1967), II: 11. "Zu deuten ist lediglich das, dessen Sinn nicht festliegt, das also vieldeutig ist."
8. Ricoeur, *"Science et idéologie,"* pp. 333–34: " . . . une idéologie est opératoire et non thématique . . . c'est à partir d'elle que nous pensons, non sur elle . . . l'idéologie est par nature une instance non critique."
9. It has been fashionable to speak of metaphysics as ontology, even in analytique philosophy and in the philosophy of science. In my paper presented at the Fifteenth International Congress of Philosophy, held in Varna, in 1974, I called Strawson's positive metaphysics "une tentation de l'esprit"; Mario Bunge's paper, published in the September 1974 issue of *Dialogue,* is entitled: *"Les présupposés et les produits métaphysiques de la science et de la technique contemporaines."* This is not the place to criticize Bunge's thesis, which leads, in my opinion, to an unacceptable conclusion: "Il n'y a pas d'incompatibilité entre science et métaphysique mais entre science superficielle et métaphysique ainsi qu'entre science profonde et métaphysique anti-scientifique" (p. 453). In other words, for Bunge, science presents a valid form of onto-

logy. In the discussion of ontology, my objections to Bunge's thesis will become evident.

10. Bunge's attempt to find a common denominator for science and philosophy fails on this ground. We read already in Aristotle's *Metaphysics* that, "since being when unspecified may mean several ways of being," logical and mathematical entites are some of the ways of being (1064 b). Hence, not only mathematics but also natural sciences will be the concern of metaphysics, since metaphysics has to examine how such beings exhibit the properties of anything as being (*Metaph.*, 11, 4). We may conclude that sciences that consider continuous quantities "must be regarded only as part of wisdom" (*Metaph.*, 1960 b). Because metaphysics makes use in its speculations of the analytic method, it does not mean that it becomes logic, i.e., the science of the a priori. On the contrary, we should say that, since the a priori is part of wisdom, scientific or positive metaphysics is part of metaphysics proper. Bunge is, then, right to say: "qu'il y a une métaphysique de la science," but he is wrong when he affirms that there is "une métaphysique scientifique."

11. This was the general purpose of Lukács's *Ontology*. Lukács's specific goal was to work out on the basis of general ontology the ontology of social being.

12. Martin Heidegger, *Was ist Metaphysik?* (Frankfurt A.M.: Klostermann, 10. ed., 1969), p. 42: Warum ist überhaupt Seiendes und nicht vielmehr Nichts? – Alexandre Kojève, *Zusammenfassende Kommentar zu den ersten sechs Kapiteln der "Phänomenologie des Geistes,"* in H.D. Fulda and D. Heinrich, eds., *Materialen zu Hegels "Phänomenologie des Geistes"* (Frankfurt A.M.: Suhrkamp, 1973), p. 149.

13. Alfred N. Whitehead, *Process and Reality* (New York: Harper and Brothers, 1960), p. 4:"... the philosophical scheme should be coherent, logical, and, in respect to its interpretation, applicable and adequate. Here 'applicable' means that some items of experience are thus interpretable, and 'adequate' means that there are no items incapable of such interpretation."

14. Béla Hegyi, *A dialógus sodrában* (Budapest: Magvető, 1978), pp. 33–36; here published in English translation for the first time, as Appendix I, pp. 124-34.

15. I found this sentence in 1979 during my visit to the Lukács Archives in the *Notes on Ethics* prepared by Lukács in view of writing a treatise on Marxist Ethics. This project became later the *Ontology*, since, as the note says "there is no ethics wihtout ontology". The *Notes on Ethics* are notes, written on any kind of paper that was at the time within the reach of Lukács's hand; some of them are so small that the writing is hardly legible. The longer and clearly legible notes are the ones written about his readings in theology; such are the notes on Augustine, Thomas Aquinas and Karl Barth.

16. Roger Garaudy, *Marxism in the Twentieth Century* (London: Collins, 1970) Lucien Goldmann, *Lukács et Heidegger* (Paris: Denoël Gonthier, 1973).

17. Cf. n. 15.

18. Karl Barth, *Die Kirschliche Dogmatik.*

19. Augustine, *Confessions,* Bk. 1, chapter 1.

20. Luchterhand, the publisher of the chapters of the *Ontology* that are so far available to us in the original German, gives the following information concerning the origin of the text: Lukács, *Ontology - Marx* (November 1972) - Der Text ist ein Kapitel der "Ontologie des gesellschaftlichen Seins" und wird später in Band 13/14 des Lukács-Werkausgabe erscheinen. Dem Text liegt eine nicht vollständige, vom Autor korrigierte Handschrift, sowie die vom Verfasser autorisierte Diktatabschrift zugrunde. Lukács, *Ontologie-Arbeit* (März 1973) -Dem Text liegt eine vom Autor stammende Handschrift, sowie eine von ihm durchgesehene Diktatabschrift zugrunde.

21. George Lukács, *Utam Marxhoz ("My Road to Marx")*, 2 vols. (Budapest: Magvetö, 1971), 1, p. 30. (My translation.)

22. Cf. *Zur Ontologie des gesellschaftlichen Seins,* part 1, *"Die gegenwärtige problemlage,"* chap. 2, *"Nikolai Hartmann's Vorstoss zu einer echten Ontologie",* p. 176. (Page citations in the text are to the manuscript of the *Ontology* in the German original and found under Lak/99-185 in the Lukács Archives, Budapest, V., Belgrád Rkp., 2.)

23. Nikolai Hartmann, *Teleologisches Denken,* (Berlin: Walter de Gruyter, 1966) 2. ed., p. 109. (My translation.)

24. Lukács, *Ontologie, Die gegenwärtige Problemlage,* p. 2. (Page citations in the text are to the manuscript.)

25. Ibid., p. 185; Nicolai Hartmann, *Philosophie der Nature* (Berlin, 1950), pp. 576, 642, quoted by Lukács.

26. This conversation is reported by Hans Dieter Bahr under the title *Zuversicht statt Hoffnung* in *Der Monat* (Feb., 1966), p. 75.

27. Lukács, *Ontologie,* chap. 2., *"Nikolai Hartmann's Vorstoss zu einer echten Ontologie,"* p. 208; Hartmann, *Teleologisches Denken,* p. 13; quoted by Lukács.

28. Lukács, *Ontologie, "Die gegenwärtige Problemlage",* Einleitung, p. 2. (My translation.) Page citations in the text are to this manuscript described in note 22.

29. Ibid., pp. 2-3-4. (My translation.)

30. Ibid., p. pp. 170-253. (My translation.)

31. Quoted in George Lukács, *Die ontologischen Grundprinzipien von Marx* (Neuwied-Darmstadt: Luchterhand, 1972), p. 4.

32. His disciples (Heller, Márkus, Vajda, Fehér), refer to their discussion with Lukács in the late 1960's and allude to Lukács's stubborn refusal to accept any technical help at the time his health was rapidly declining. They quote him saying: "I have to clean my own dirty laundry." (*"Notes and Commentary: Notes on Lukács' Ontology"* by Ferenc Fehér, Agnes Heller, György Márkus and Mihály Vajda in *Telos* (Fall 1976) no. 29, pp. 161-62.) One may wonder whether the refusal of their aid was not only the cover up of Lukács's determination to leave the Ontology unchanged and incomplete since he had no time for a complete reorganization of the material. In the preface of his *Utam Marxhoz* (*"My Road to Marx",* p. 30.) dated October 1969, he wrote: "The first manuscript of this ontology was ready last year, but careful examination revealed that it needed thorough rethinking and revision before it could be published." (My translation.)

33. Lukács, *Ontologischen Grundlagen;* see Appendix II. (Page references in the text are to this translation.)

34. Lukács, *Utam Marxhoz* (*"My Road to Marx"*) 2 vols. (Budapest: Magvető, 1971), II, pp. 542-64.

35. P.136: The Marxian ontology eliminates from the Hegelian all logical-deductive and teleological elements of historico-evolutionary nature . . . the decisive philosophical intervention of Marx was to overcome the logical-philosophical idealism of Hegel and to point theoretically and practically towards the conception of a materialistic and historical ontology.

36. Cf. Georg Lukács, *Hegels falsche und echte Ontologie* (Berlin-Neuwied: Luchterhand, 1971), p. 11: Die Afuklärung, wie alle ihre Vorgänger, scheitert daran, dass sie das Fundiert-sein jener auf dieser allzu einheitlich, allzu homogen, allzu direct fasst und das ontologische Prinzip der *qualitativen Differenz* innerhalb der letzthinnigen Einheit gedanklich nicht zu ergreifen vermag . . . Es ist klar, dass die starr-dogmatische Einheitlichkeit des damals herrschenden mechanistischen Materialismus zu dieser Differenzierung höchst ungeeignet ist. [Italics mine.]

37. Lukács, *Utam Marxhoz* (*"My Road to Marx"*), 2 vols. (Budapest: Magvető, 1971): "Heidegger's thought taken as the confession of a bourgeois of the 1920s is not without interest"

(2:117). "Now, if we present in a brief survey how the problems of everyday life and thinking appear in Heidegger in a distorted and impoverished form, some may protest against our classification of Heidegger among the romantic critics of the capitalistic culture" (2:344). "Existentialism as the dominating trend among bourgeois intellectuals today . . . Nietzsche, the leading philosopher of the imperialistic reactionalism" (2:98). (My translation.)

38. "In Marx, the point of departure is neither the atom, as in the materialism of antiquity, nor, as in Hegel, abstract being as such . . . For Marx, the existent entities must be objective (i.e., objects) and at the same time active and passive components of a concrete totality" (VP, p. 149; Appendix II, p. 136).

39. VP, p. 163; Appendix II, p. 148.

40. "Marx conceived consciousness as a late product of the ontological evolution of matter." (VP, p. 149; Appendix II, p. 137.

41. VP, pp. 151, 158–159, 160–161; Appendix II, pp. 138, 144-5, 146-7; cf. Lukács, "*The dialectic of Labour: Beyond Causality and Teleology,*" trans. A.W. Gucinski, *Telos,* No. 6, Fall 1970, pp. 162–74.

42. VP, p. 152; Appendix II, p. 139. While asserting the teleological causation of labor, Lukács also maintains the existence of a necessity without teleology. Of course, teleology humanized excludes transcendental teleology; Lukács does not claim indeed that we are in complete control of our "world". The social process is a causal process with its own laws — and it never follows any objective aims; one has to act under the threat of perishing. (VP, pp. 157, 154; Appendix II, pp. 143, 141).

43. " . . . die Notwendigkeit aufhört, mechanisch-spontan zu wirken . . . Die teleologische Genesis hat naturgemäss wichtige Konsequenzen für alle gesellschaftlichen Prozesse" (VP, pp. 157, 156; Appendix II, p. 143).

44. VP, p. 150; Appendix II, p. 137.

45. Aristotle, *Metaph.,* K, 1, 1059a23: "first principles are not contraries."

46. See the table of contents of his projected *Ontology* in *Hegels falsche und echte Ontologie* (Neuwied-Berlin: Luchterhand, 1971), pp. 127–28.

47. VP, 154; Appendix II, p. 141. Cf. Peter Demetz, *Marx, Engels, and the Poets* (Chicago University Press, 1967), chap. 8, "*George Lukács as a Theoretician of Literature*". Cf. also George Kline, "*Impressions of the Man and His Ideas,*" in *Problems of Communism,* chap. "*Lukács in Retrospect,*" 21 (1972): 66: "On the whole I found Lukács' 'Hegelian' discussion of Vermittlung and Vermittlungsfelder interesting and congenial. But from time to time the Engels-Lenin side of Lukács showed through in a disconcerting way, as for example when he spoke — quite seriously — of the cognitive and artistic 'reflection' (Widerspiegelung) of social or natural reality. At one point he listed a galaxy of Elizabethan dramatists who were highly esteemed by their contemporaries — such as Marlowe, Ford, and Webster — and went on to assert that of all the Elizabethans only Shakespeare was still a living force in English literature and culture . . . 'because his reflection of Elizabethan social reality was the correct one' and their 'reflections' of that reality were somehow 'less correct.' "

48. All page citations in the text are to the English version of the Notes published in *Telos,* No. 29, Fall 1976, pp. 160–81, under the title: "*Notes and Commentary: Notes on Lukács' Ontology.*" The Italian version appeared in *Aut-Aut,* January-June, 1977.

49. January-June 1977.

50. The "Notes" were originally written in Hungarian and relate the events that marked the last

years and even the last days of the "grand" old man. Would it not have been natural to publish them first in a Hungarian philosophical journal so that others, who have also witnessed those events could have added their own observations?

51. This opinion is confirmed by conversations I had with those who were close to Lukács during his last years and also by the account of his disciples published in *Telos* (cf. note 32). A *Prolegomena* is an introduction to a work; it cannot be a reformulation of its main tenets.

52. Cf. *Spiegel*, 14 June 1971.

53. However, the objections to the *Ontology* can be retraced in the printed text (in the chapters on *Marx* and *Die Arbeit*), and I shall indicate some of the places. But it must be noted that often they sum up a general tendency in Lukács's work, as in *Alienation*, therefore, the disappearance of the manuscript they refer to should not suggest that the disciples base their criticism on a different version of the *Ontology*. The change of pagination is probably due to the efforts of the editors to establish a sequence of the chapters.

54. Cf. *Ontologie, Die ontologischen Grundprinzipien von Marx* (Darmstadt-Neuwied: Luchterhand, 1972), p. 136. Lukács develops here the notion of *Ungleichmässigkeit*, i.e., to what extent an economic process in spite of its necessary laws leads to various end results depending on the intervention of subjective factors. "Es ist also eine ontologisch wohlbegründete Tatsache, dass es objektiv revolutionäre Situationen geben kann, die ungelöst bleiben, weil der subjektive Faktor nicht entsprechend herangereift ist, wie auch Volksexplosionen möglich sind, denen kein hinreichende objektiven Krisenmomente entsprechen. Es bedarf keiner ausführlichen Erläuterung, dass diese Sachlage ein wichtiges Moment der Ungleichmässigkeit in der gesellschaftlich-geschichtlichen Entwicklung bildet. Man denke bloss an das zweimalige Versagen des subjektiven Factors im modernen Deutschland (1848 und 1918)."

55. Cf. Georg Lukács, *Ontologie*, Part II, *Die Arbeit* (Neuwied-Darmstadt: Luchterhand, 1973), pp. 33–34.

56. Ibid., pp. 35–36.

57. Ibid., p. 34.

58. Marx, in MEGA I, 5. 533; MEW 3. 5. (Quoted by Lukács, *Die Arbeit*, p. 35.)

59. Georg Klauss and Manfred Buhr, eds., *Philosophies Wörterbuch*, 2 vols. (Leipzig: VEB Bibiliographical Institut, 1970), 1:197.

60. Ibid., p. 198.

61. Cf. "Notes", p. 175; see also Lukács, *Ontologie, Die Arbeit*, pp. 127, 152.

62. "Notes", p. 175.

63. Ibid.

64. Karl Marx, *Werke* (Berlin: Dietz), 18:33. Quoted in the "Notes" p. 180.

65. Georg Lukács, *Ontology, Prolegomena*, in Hungarian (Budapest; Magvetö, 1976), p. 11. (My translation.)

66. Lukács, *Ontologie, Die Arbeit*, p. 128. (My translation.)

67. Ibid., pp. 11–12: Engels weist jedoch mit derselben Entscheidenheit darauf hin, dass trotz solcher Vorbereitungen hier doch ein Sprung vorliegt, der sich nicht mehr innerhalb des Organischen abspielt, sondern ein prinzipielles, qualitatives, ontologisches Hinausgehen darüber bedeutet; . . . jeder Sprung eine qualitative und strukturelle Veränderung im Sein bedeutet . . . Dieser Bruch mit der normalen Kontinuität der Entwicklung macht das Wesen des Sprunges aus, nicht die zeitlich plötzliche oder allmähliche Entstehen der neuen Seinsform. . . Es muss nur erwähnt werden, dass Engels hier, mit Recht, Gesellschaftlichkeit und Sprache unmittelbar aus der Arbeit ableitet."

68. "Notes, pp. 174–75; e.g., Consciousness as nonexistent; the positionings of consciousness are such nonexisting acts.

69. Ibid., p. 172.

Chapter 5

1. Lucien Goldmann, *Lukács et Heidegger* (Paris: Denoël-Gonthier, 1973). (Translations are mine.) Page citations in the text are to this edition.
2. Georg Lukács, *Ontologie,* Part 1, *"Die gegenwärtige Problemlage"* introduction, p. 2. (My translation.)
3. Martin Heidegger, *What is Metaphysics?* introduction (1949); trans. W. Kaufmann, in Walter Kaufmann, *Existentialism from Dostoevski to Sartre* (New York: Meridian Books, 1969). Trans. Kaufmann.
4. Martin Heidegger, *Sein und Zeit,* trans. John Macquarrie and Edward Robinson (New York and Evanston: Harper and Row, 1962), p. 1: "Our aim in the following treatise is to work out the question of the meaning of Being and to do so concretely."
5. "The Interpretation of *time* as possible horizon for any understanding whatsoever of Being." (Ibid.)
6. Ibid., pp. 375-76.
7. Ibid., p. 376.
8. Lucien Goldmann, *Lukács et Heidegger,* p. 98.
9. *"Notes and Commentary: Notes on Lukács's Ontology, " Telos,* No. 29, Fall 1976, pp. 160-81.
10. See note 6 to Chapter IV.
11. Goldmann, *Lukács et Heidegger,* p. 105.
12. *Telos,* No. 10, Winter 1971, p. 93.
13. Heidegger, *Sein und Zeit,* p. 437.
14. Heidegger, *Was ist Metaphysik?* (Frankfurt A.M.: Klostermann, 1969), introduction p. 21.
15. Heidegger, *Sein und Zeit,* p. 68.
16. Ibid., p. 69.
17. Heidegger, *Was ist Metaphysik?* p. 21.
18. Heidegger, *Sein und Zeit,* p. 437.
19. Ibid., p. 38.
20. George Lukács, *Utam Marxhoz ("My Road to Marx"),* 2 vols. (Budapest: Magvetö, 1971), 2:101. (My translation.) Page citations in the text are to this edition.
21. Heidegger, *Sein und Zeit,* pp. 63-4.
22. Lukács, *Ontology,* Part 1, *Die gegenwärtige Problemlage,* p. 97.
23. Heidegger, *Lettre sur l'Humanisme,* bilingual edition, trans. Roger Munier (Paris Aubier, Montaigne, 1964), p. 50. (My translation.)
24. Ibid., p. 56; cf. p. 60: In "Sein und Zeit (S. 42) steht gesperrt der Satz: "Das 'Wesen' des Daseins liegt in seiner Existenz". See also Lukács, *Ontology,* Part 2, *Die Arbeit,* p. 12: Es muss erwähnt werden, dass Engels here, mit Recht Gesellschaftlichkeit und Sprache unmittelbar aus der Arbeit ableitet. Cf. Karl Marx, *Economic and Philosophical Manuscripts,* trans. T.B. Bottomore, in Erich Fromm, *Marx's Concept of Man* (New York: Ungar, 1977), p. 183.
25. Andrew Feenberg, *"Reification and Antinomies of Socialist Thought," Telos,* No. 10, Winter 1971, pp. 93-118.
26. *Salmagundi,* No. 13, 1970, pp. 4-35.

27. Feenberg, *"Reification and Antinomies,"* p. 97.
28. Ibid., p. 101.
29. Ibid., p. 102.
30. Cf. ibid., n. 16.
31. Ibid.

Chapter 6

1. Cf. André Lalande, *Vocabulaire technique et critique de la philosophie (Paris: Presse Universitaire de France, 1972), 11. ed., pp. 759–60; Herders Kleines Philosophisches Wörterbuch,* eds. Max Müller and Alois Halder (Freiburg im Bresgau: Herder Verlag, 11, ed., 1969), pp. 129–30.
2. Georg Klaus and Manfred Buhr, eds., *Philosophisches Wörterbuch,* 2 vols. (Leipzig: VEB Bibliographisches Institut, 1970), vol. 2:828–30.
3. George Lukács, *History and Class Consciousness,* trans. Rodney Livingstone (Cambridge, Massachusetts: The MIT Press, 1976), p. 46.
4. Ibid., p. 47.
5. Cf. Chapter 3, *Praxis and Theory: Tactics and Ethics.*
6. Lukács, *History and Class Consciousness,* pp. 49–50.
7. Ibid., p. 51.
8. Cf. Chapter IV, *"The Vienna Paper."*
9. Cf. Béla Hegyi, *A dialógus sodrában* (Budapest: Magvetö, 1978), p. 48; see Appendix II, p. for the English translation.
10. Max Scheler, *Formalism in Ethics and Non-Formal Ethics of Values* trans. Manfred Frings and Roger L. Funk (Evanston: Northwestern University Press, 1973).

Appendix 1   AN INTERVIEW WITH GEORGE LUKÁCS*

George Lukács was the first to launch the idea of the dialogue [between the state and the churches]. In a conference held during the summer of 1956, he drew attention to the fact that "some outstanding theologians no longer wish to brush aside Marxism as a variation of vulgar materialism, but feel the necessity of a serious debate centering on its problems. The "conciliatory attitude" of Catholicism offers an opportunity for entering into contact, for starting a dialogue or a debate which five or ten years earlier seemed unthinkable."

Lukács not only pressed for dialogue but was actively involved in it himself. He was open for discussion from all quarters. Though he never tired in arguing his own position, he always respected the opinions of the other party, particularly when these convictions were grounded in a living faith and an intellectual orientation, and did not involve a flagrant contradiction between faith and act.

Today, at 85, he is the most famous man in Hungary. Everyone — Marxist and non-Marxist, believer or indifferent — is eager to hear his views.

At the beginning of our conversation he reminds me: "I do not give interviews, but you may take notes."

Later on, he softens his attitude: "I do not mind if you publish everything, provided it is not in the form of an interview. During the past month, so many journalists came to see me, that I have had enough of them. After all, I am not a movie star, nor am I a Nixon who has a stereotyped answer for all questions, that is, an "image." You are a writer, solve this problem . . ."

The Philosopher and the Politician

It is rare for one person to be at the same time theoretician and politician. In Marx's opinion, ideology is needed, first, to make social conflicts conscious, and, second, to serve in the struggle for their resolution. With minor reservations, the same applies to politics. However, social conflicts arise at

*Taken from Béla Hegyin, *A dialógus sodrában* (Budapest: Magvetö, 1978), and published with the permission of the author. My translation — E.J. Editorial insertions made by the translator appear in square brackets; those made by Hegyi appear in parentheses.

different levels and reach different proportions. Therefore, it is not mere chance that Lenin, the politician, set for himself the task of solving concrete contradictions. To accomplish this he endeavored to select (out of the chain of events) the crucial link, the grasping of which would make him master of the whole chain. On the other hand, the task of a thinker or of a philosopher is not to concern himself with problems belonging properly to the sphere of the politician, but to resolve the great theoretical problems of an age. Without doubt, he renders in this way a great service to politicians, without necessarily making it possible for them to trade in this principle immediately for ideas applicable to their tactics. The great theoreticians of Marxism were at the same time great political leaders. The best Marxists gave priority to science and theory; tactics and strategy were the natural outcome of Marxist analysis. Stalin was unable to fulfill this double role of Marxist theoretician and leader of the working class. Stalinism suffocated Marxist theory: he forged tactics and strategy from a current political situation, then he did the worst thing one can do by dressing it in theoretical garments.

His Place in Philosophy

I am not a politician, and it is also certain that I am not a new Marx: Marx read reality; and I am reading Marx. Let us not confuse the standards . . . Perhaps the workers' movement will give birth to a new Marx, since neither Engels nor Lenin can be compared to Marx in respect to the wealth of his thought. But I dare to affirm that I understood Marx best. My role can be summed up thus: to trace the direction of theoretical work for those who come after me. If I have succeeded in discovering the right method, then I may say that I lived well, that it was worth living. Whether I was right or not will only be known twenty years after my death. There are no thinkers who have judged all questions and situations correctly. Marx is the only one who was right in most cases . . .

The Beginning

Marx's intellectual evolution is uninterrupted. I cannot make the same claim about my own. I must admit, without trying to embellish the story, that I came to Marxism relatively late, at the age of 35, though I first became interested in Marx during my secondary-school years. My ideals exercised a decisive influence on my life. It matters, especially at a certain age, whom we choose as models. The decisive influence [Endre] Ady [famous Hungarian poet] exercised on my life culminated during the relentless struggle against the Hungarian state of affairs and, through this, against everything that prevailed in his time. I had already longed for such a conception of life in my youth, without being able to articulate my feelings. For a long time, in spite of several rereadings, I was unable to appreciate the degree to which this aspect is manifest in Marx, so I could not make use of his criticism of the Kantian and Hegelian philosophical systems. What I could not grasp in Marx had become evident to me in the attitude of Ady, the poet. Since first meeting Ady, I could not free myself from his restlessness; it haunted me and remained on the surface in all my thinking, although for a long time I was unable to raise it to the level of consciousness in a manner befitting its importance. I was separated from the twentieth century and the West by my aversion towards Western culture. I was convinced that translating the writers of the Occident into Hungarian would not help Hungary. When I was first leaning towards admitting into my world view the internal transformation of man as the principal factor in bringing about social reform, I incorporated into this world view the great Russian revolutionary writers Dostoevski and Tolstoi. This coincided with my conviction that, from the methodological point of view, ethics raised itself above the philosophy of history. This idea became the ideological basis of my involvement in the world and it has grown out of my Ady experience. I do not deny that at this time religious ideology had an equally strong influence on me, especially the medieval reform movement.

The fact that through Ervin Szabó I got acquainted with Georges Sorel and the unionists contributed to the shaping of the Hegel–Ady–Dostoevski influence into a world view that I felt, at that time, to be revolutionary. This revolutionary conception without revolution became the ideological basis of my friendship with Béla Balázs, whose apartment was the meeting place of the friends who, at the end of the First World War, founded the Free School of Human Sciences. Both in the West and at home, the importance of this (school) has been overestimated, because here I could not find answers to the new questions that were about to arise, namely, "Where to go? What is the solution?" With its members—Károly Mannheim, Arnold Hauser, Károly Tolnay, Antal Frigyes—I got along well if we disregard ideological differences. My romantic criticism of capitalism faced a crisis. Although in my general conception of the world I was already moving away from Hegel and towards Marx, this change was noticeable only in the uneasy coexistence of the Hegelian doctrine regarding the striving for internal transformation and the Marxist revolutionary trend.

I must stress that my idealism never manifested itself with more passionate intransigence than during this transitory period, when I was consciously striving to surpass it. Step by step I approached the point where I was able to overcome the dualism of materialism and idealism in my thought and reach a throughgoing Marxist-materialist world view. It was only during my stay in

Moscow following my emigration from Vienna in 1919 that I succeeded in framing questions from the proper perspective.

Theoretical Problems

We mark the beginning of a real Marxist renaissance. More and more people recognize that Marxism provides the only workable solution to the current world crisis. If we wish to guarantee its authority in all fields, then we have to endeavor to transform it in such a way that it may be respected by all. The method of Marxism is the right method to solve the problems of socialism and capitalism without resorting to violence. But above all, we have to reach the proper understanding of the essence of Marxism and also of the great changes that have occurred since Marx. The precondition of this understanding is the continuation of the work of Marx in every domain of the Marxist theory, starting from the point at which Marx left off in 1883, and carefully analyzing in Marx's spirit events up to our own time.

During these past eighty years, many changes have occurred in the fields of the natural sciences, technology, production, economics, and also in the structure of capitalism, which were not foreseeable in Marx's lifetime. Contemporary Marxists have not yet given a satisfactory scientific explanation to account, for example, for the intermittence in the cyclical crises of capitalism, although change goes on in capitalism as well as elsewhere. There are still people today who, opening the newspaper, expect to read of the final collapse of capitalism in America and the attendant socialist uprising. An equally misguided view contends that the situation has changed so much that capitalism can no longer be called capitalism. Generally speaking, the Marxian laws are valid for capitalism, but require adjustments. It is crucial for socialism also that we see the world, including capitalism with all its characteristics, from the Marxist standpoint. But we have to be cautioned that without proper analysis of the economic process — all evaluation is only popular wisdom. I see in tacticism, that is a sort of opportunism, the obstacle to the revival of theoretical work. Instead of applying intelligence to the improvement and criticism of practice, we subjugate it to momentary needs. Our opportunism manifests itself still in another manner: even now, 120 years after the *Communist Manifesto* — and 50 years after the establishment of the first Marxist state — we have not yet published Marx's complete works. Several papers written by Marx — among them the notes he prepared for the *Capital* — are covered with dust in inaccessible archives. This is inexcusable.

Socialist society is now facing the task of establishing a qualitatively new democracy, up to these days unknown. I reject the application of bourgeois democracy to socialist society. This would not resolve any problem. I cannot tell now what this democracy will be like, but I remind you of the first days of the soviet revolution, of the soviet of workers, peasants, and soliders, of the democracy of workers, peasants, and soldiers. I speak about this *in abstracto*. We should attempt a new theoretical elaboration of this democracy, adapting it to the exigencies of our times, so that this democracy may arise in accord with the needs of our society. I always opposed bureaucracy and manipulation both in the arts and in politics. I am convinced that it is the bringing about of a "little" democracy that solves problems of our everyday life and that in turn leads to the dismantling of bureaucracy. The study of Marxism should prepare the way for the organization of such a democracy.

Praxis itself stresses the urgency of elaborating a Marxist ethics. I am not convinced that economic progress is all-determining—that the abundance of material goods and the steady improvement of living standards will solve all problems and will automatically produce communism. Men make their own history, but not under circumstances that they have chosen. Ethics in the sense of an autonomous science, as it is conceived by bourgeois philosophy, does not exist. Man adapts himself actively to his environment and the task of ethics is to elucidate the history, the essence, and the evaluation of human activities. In my opinion, this is a fundamental philosophical task. The existence or nonexistence of certain categories is a very important question. The construction of a categorial system which is capable of accounting for the reality of what we consider real is indispensable for Marxism, if it is to successfully combat the aberrations that arise from its own materialistic characteristics, and if it is to intensify its criticism of existentialist and neopositivist positions. We have to elaborate a Marxist ontology such that it contains the unity of historical and dialectical materialism. This enterprise must be carried out on the basis of a conception that is both historical (in nature)—without falling into the error of relativism—and systematic—without betraying history. Until this task is completed, Marxists will not be equipped to fight, for example, irrationalist tendencies à la Marcuse, or the neopositivists, and will be specially handicapped in combatting the pseudorationalistic views of structuralism.

What Is Human

I shrink away from this term because each and everyone understands something different by it. The term "human" has become fashionable phraseology. Marx elevated the essence of this term in his theses on Feuerbach: every man should live a life befitting the species, a life that allows the full development of individuality. Whether one's activity makes one human or inhuman depends on the needs one wishes to satisfy. Seeking the satisfaction of unreal needs—private property, graft—renders one inhuman. On the contrary, the satisfaction of real needs makes one progressively more human. Man's most essential need is to be a man as much as possible, and to develop his own and his fellows' humanity. This is the way towards the development of human needs and this is how we realize in ourselves the totality of our essence. In the past the great reformers of our culture were mostly idealist preachers or idealist humanists. Consider only Savonarola, Rousseau, Robespierre, and Tolstoi. These reformers initiated the shaping of human life "from above": soul, ethics, and the transformation of man's inner life were meant to be the levers that should have transformed and thus renewed completely the exterior conditions of life of humanity.

Socialist humanism embraces the life of all intelligent men and not only that of a class. It intends to transform life through freedom acquired in constant activity. According to Marx, we evolved from natural being into human person: from relatively superior animal to human species; to humanity through the inner and outer transformation of social reality. He defines the realm of freedom as such: "human effort which is an end in itself," which is rich enough that both the individual and society recognize it as an end in itself.

But the condition for freeing the social road for the realization of human activity as an end in itself is that the work must come entirely under the domination of mankind in such a way that work be not "merely the means to survive" but the first necessity. Humanity has to pass beyond the constraint of its own reproduction. Marx considers all the consequences of historical development and concludes that real history can start only with communism as a higher form of socialism. Communism for Marx is not a utopian vision of a future actuality; on the contrary, it is the beginning of the unfolding of truly human forces which were created and further improved in a paradoxical fashion as the most important means towards becoming man.

Progress

I believe in progress, even if it does not mean an overall improvement. The uneven nature of progress does not exclude, in spite of its negative aspects, positive sides. The road to the understanding of reality is much longer than some would imagine it; in fact, it has no end. One can look after oneself using one's opportunities; one has the choice. One can make use even of one's misfortunes. Each man makes his own history.

Contemporary Literature

Literature nowadays is too practical; I could even say that it moves on the level of best-sellers. I do not see such geniuses as Thomas Mann and Goethe. The favorite writers — Joyce, Green — are good writers but they are far from being great. Our literature is lacking exactly that which made literature in earlier days great, for instance, the literature of Enlightenment from Voltaire to Diderot and Rousseau. Of course, there are exceptions: some parts of Hochhut's plays, the Antigons of Berlin, Böll's *Billiards at Nine-Thirty*, or *The Old Lady* by Dürenmatt. But even here, one has to make a distinction. I do not think any of Dürenmatt's [other] works come close to *The Old Lady*. Although our literature does not see its mission in the way it was defined since Homer and the Greek tragedies, it imagines that it creates something new: in this it deludes itself. It looks as if literature had renounced its real possibilities, which are obviously not direct possibilities. I mean, it was not necessary that Diderot's readers destroy the Bastille; but I am convinced that, without Rousseau and Diderot, the new ideology which led to the destruction of the Bastille would not have been born. However, it is not only literature that neglects its role as transformer of society; science and philosophy do the same. I do not consider the commitment of writers to be decisive. However, this does not mean that I would despise it. But one should not disregard the fact that there were great writers such as Lessing and Heine, etc., who refused to take a political stand or to belong to a party. At the same time, Heine's poem "Deutschland" is a much more radical condemnation of Germany than any politician could have formulated at that time. Therefore, I am convinced that the more truly great poetry and great literature represent man and the more penetrating the analysis they make of the problems facing man, the more decisive the role they play in preparing ideologically the transformation and development of society.

Literature cannot, therefore, give up its role of offering perspectives to mankind. Of course, this is nothing new. We find this already in *Iphigenia* and to some degree in *The Iliad* when Priam comes to Achilles to ask for Hector's body, an act totally in contradiction with the norms of this age.

Nowadays, the fight against alienation is, indeed, a fight for the conservation and development of human values, and this fight is fought under the most favorable economic and particularly unfavorable social conditions. This is where literature can accomplish more than it ever did.

The Crisis of Religion

The death of the state is far away; so is that of religion. Nowadays there are still millions of believers, and the Marxists cannot ignore this fact. It is true that religion is undergoing in our days an unprecedented crisis because the application of its commandments to everyday life has become problematic.

Nobody knows how deep this crisis is or how long it will last. But one thing is certain: it is not yet the absolute or final crisis of religion. I am a radical atheist and I am convinced that history will confirm my opinion. We cannot ignore the fact that religion has profound influence on a number of Marxists. Some, like Bloch, Garaudy, and Ernst Fisher, openly play a game with religion and would like to come to a compromise with it. I disapprove of such an attitude because it blurs the distinction between the two conceptions of life and thus misleads people.

At the same time, we can affirm that the great problems of our age have had an impact on a large number of believers; the great events of world history have left their mark on them, for religion is not an isolated phenomenon, nor is it abstract ideology taught by a lonely professor from his chair: it is rather a concrete social phenomenon. Religion relies on millions of believers who participate in a sociohistorical life and who are constantly influenced by more or less important historical events. World historical events have an impact on the masses of Catholics also. This influence is visible in the attitude of those who try to bridge the differences between the Catholic dogma and the conditions of life of workers, farmers, and intellectuals, and who try to solve this antagonism by reinterpreting religion.

Marxism and Christianity

Today, because the crisis of religion affects the majority of believers, they have become more sensitive towards Marxism, and I would not like to underestimate their cooperation in the politicosocial sphere. What I doubt is that nowadays a Thomas Münzer or a Savonarola could exist. In Luther's age, after the Reformation, the consciousness of the masses was shaped by religion for the last time. In the sixteenth century, Catholicism underwent a serious crisis because of the Reformation. Catholicism, founded on feudal ideology, seemed to be losing the struggle against the Protestant churches, which grew out of the soil of early capitalism. The social meaning of the Counter-Reformation consisted in the following: it helped the Catholic church divest itself of feudalism, which sought its support by any means, and then it established a close relation with early capitalism and its contemporary political system — the monarchy. Catholicism survived the crises of the sixteenth and seventeenth centuries and succeeded in creating the conditions for its [own] further development.

Let us only recall the merits of Barth, which are, in my opinion, very great. During the Hitler regime he stood up against fascism, and as a consequence of his resistance faithful Chrisitans turned away from those who served Hitler. But I am not sure whether Barth's initiative could be called a revolutionary movement. Because the religious aspect of life and its Christian

valuation are losing ground progressively, I do not believe in the decisive influence of Christianity. However, this judgment does not prevent me from
recognizing the human value of certain people such as Simon Weil. Her fate is
characteristic of outstanding personalities. Social circumstances occasionally
produce problems that may find in any age an individual solution. Although
she was in contact with other social movements, Simone Weil followed a very
peculiar path. But she herself cannot be called a "movement" and never will
become such. In countries where a movement starts, and it is limited to the
field of theology—for instance, in France under the influence of Teilhard de
Chardin—it has an impact on social and political evolution only to the extent
that it removes the barrier that hinders believers from joining any progressive
movement. In this respect, the role [of those religious leaders] is definitely
positive.

The Attempt of Teilhard de Chardin

Last year a translation of one of my articles came out in *Világosság*
(*"Light"*). It stresses the opposition of Marxism and religion on every issue. I
hold that all philosophical attempts that try to mediate between Marxism and
Christianity theoretically are unsound. Marxism is far removed from all
transcendence. The attempt of Teilhard de Chardin to reconcile the two conceptions of the world is a failure. I cannot imagine reaching the point where we
could find a synthesis between Thomas Aquinas and Marx. I do not question
Chardin's achievements in paleontology; nevertheless, in inventing a nonexistent physics and showing an evolution of forces that culminate in Christ, he
definitely cheated. This method reminds me of a Jewish anecdote about garlic
and chocolate that was fashionable in Pest during the 1920s. In itself, each one
is agreeable, the chocolate and the garlic. But the two together? Teilhard is a
typical example of chocolate and garlic. My skepticism is not the expression of
my indifference towards the present age. We continue to observe a whole
series of religious traditions which have lost their importance even for believers
and in such a way that both, believers and nonbelievers, have the same attitude
towards them. However, we should not overestimate their social importance.

The Dialogue

I am entirely in favor of dialogue, even today, but without overestimating
its importance. If, at this moment, a debate with a leftist Catholic started,
without prior reflexion and preparation, we would achieve no result whatsoever. The dialogue can be successful only on the practical level, but not on
the theoretical. It should not be turned into an idol. The West uses it as
material for propaganda. The dialogue occasionally can be a means among in-

dividuals for coming to an agreement; but it cannot be a collective aim, as Western ideologists would have it. It is very important to carry on the dialogue with Christians, but, in order to be useful, it must be exempt from demagogy and it must be theoretically sound. In the course of history, the Church's relationship to society demonstrates a series of compromises. the church adapted itself for centuries even to feudalism (Thomas Aquinas); it later existed in peace with capitalism. Today a modus vivendi is a necessary condition for the survival of the church—that is, the church has to reconcile itself with socialism, and it has to adapt itself to the new system. There are many signs that point in this direction. Dutschke, the German student leader, enjoys the support of several theologians. Divorce is not permitted in Italy, but even some church leaders consider this senseless in the twentieth century, and are of the opinion that the church has to give in to the fact that the dissolution of marriage must be accepted in a modern society. All these facts reflect the adaptation of the church to contemporary society. If, at times, the church supports the Marxist position on certain issues, I do not see why Marxists could not support the church in turn. In practice, this means for me that I should be actively engaged in any reform movement: if I were Dutch, I would fight against celibacy, if I were Italian, I would go in now for the introduction of a law governing religion, etc., and I would support everywhere the creation of a common front between Marxists and the Christian left.

The starting point of the dialogue—or an ideology for a transitory period—consists in understanding that there is a common goal that all of us equally pursue, and for this reason the discussion of social problems is in the interest of all. The Marxist position must be unambiguous and objective. Humanity is wavering between two extremes: this means either the submission to Stalinism and along with it to dogmatism, or the irresponsible acceptance of Western criticism. Marxism is neither the one nor the other.

Postscript

(Life is the scene of activity for both Marxism and Christianity. However, death seems to definitely terminate this temporary cooperation and the human forms of mutual aid. Materialism limits here, to the earth, all activity, and opens no gate for man towards the infinite. Relgion, when promising the continuation of earthly existence, places man above the world and it awakens in us the hope of an existence beyond the world.) Death for me is a purely biological fact, a characteristic of all living organisms; whatever is generated faces corruption, has a beginning and an end in the interplay of the forces of nature. But in the case of man, even death means something more [than corruption]. Since we are social beings, we wish to attribute even to death a special rank, a peculiar meaning. Even the ancients tried to transform death into a social event. For instance, the stoics taught that whenever man happened to be in circumstances unworthy of his status as man he had the right to commit suicide. This is how death has gained social importance and has become a social factor. Socrates, Savonarola, Jeanne d'Arc died a social death, too, not only a biological one. Socrates drank the hemlock, although his friends had prepared his escape. He accepted the sentence of death that was imposed upon him, because only in this way could he remain what he was. Savonarola did not retract his teachings either, because he would have been in contradiction with himself; rather, he accepted being burned at the stake. Jeanne d'Arc was also given an opportunity to betray her mission. She could have attested that her visions were lies. But how could she have reconciled such an act with her conscience? The martyrs and saints of the church, too, lived and acted in the same way. This was the reason why they were held in such esteem for centuries and had an influence on the masses. I myself could not have acted otherwise when I hid from the White Terror after the fall of the dictatorship of the proletariate. The house whose attic was my hiding place was searched several times. Each time, I put to myself the question: What happens if they find me? I swore allegiance to the Workers Council of 1919 and I was responsible to it. Therefore, if necessary, I shall face death. I shall not abandon my faith. I shall not deny my acts. For me, this attitude constitutes the essence of ethics. The trial of our humanity: to be consequent in our actions; if necessary, face death for them. It is not true that we have no choice; we do, always and everywhere. It is true that this attitude is not easy to bear. If we are determined to be consequent up to the end in decisive moments of our life, death is transformed into an everlasting value. Biological death is raised to another level: it attains a socioethical importance. We are saved—to whatever *Weltanschauung* we belong—by the socioethical death. [We achieve this] when we can leave this life with the comforting idea that we have not lived in vain, that we remained faithful to ourselves, to our convictions, and that we were useful to others as much as it was in our power to be so.

(When Marx was asked about his human confession of faith, he answered: Whatever is human is not alien to me. How would you formulate it yourself?) I would say what I wrote in Heinrich Böll's notebook, quoting Peer Gynt, who discovered a profound truth—the difference between man and elf: " . . . outside under the blue sky man says: 'Man, be yourself!' But among us the same is said differently: 'Elf, let you always suffice to yourself.' "

(1970)

Appendix 2   The "Vienna Paper": The Ontological Foundations of Human Thinking and Action by George Lukács

[*Translator's Note.* In all ideologies directed specifically towards praxis there is a very noticeable weakness—the lack of rigor in the employment of terms. In spite of the subtlety of Lukács his style is not exempt from this defect. There is another, equally embarrassing for the translator—his wordiness. Lukács's terms are almost always redundant. The translator has the choice of reproducing them, which makes the English style similar to second-rate German, or cutting them out in hope of improving Lukács's style, thus omitting what some may consider subtleties. The translator has committed both errors and accepts responsibility for them. However, he has never changed the basic terminology. Passages in brackets and in italics are summaries of paragraphs that were repetitious and did not seem to add anything essential to the text.

This paper was originally prepared for delivery at the Fourteenth International Congress of Philosophy, held in Vienna, September 1968. My translation has been made on the basis of the manuscript found in the Lukács Archives under the number LAK/421 and published in *ad lectores* 8, pp. 148-64 (Neuwied-Berlin: Luchterhand, 1968), and its Hungarian version by János Kis, printed in George Lukács, *Utam Marxhoz* ("*My Road to Marx*"), 2 vols. (Budapest: Magvető, 1971), 2:542-64.—The translation has been authorized by Ferenc Jánossy, heir to Lukács's copyright.— E.J.]

We face two difficulties if we wish to classify, even superficially, in one conference, the most general principles of this problem-complex. On the one hand, we should have a critical examination of the problem as it stands today; on the other hand, we should expound at least the fundamental structure of a new ontology. In order to tackle the second and more important problem, we have to abandon even the abridged exposition of the first question. We are all aware of the fact that in the last decades neopositivism, a more radical form of older epistemological tendencies that considered any ontological questioning as nonscientific, was the absolute ruling force. This tendency dominated not only the philosophical sphere, but also the world of praxis. If once someone seriously analyzes the theoretical leitmotiv of contemporary political, military, and economic tendencies, it will become obvious that, consciously or unconsciously, these tendencies are determined by neopositivistic thinking. The quasi-omnipotence of neopositivism rests on this ground: if one day the confrontation with reality issues in an open crisis, this will provoke a great revolution both in political and economic life and in our way of philosophizing. Since we are only at the beginning of this process, these remarks should suffice.

In our paper, we will not discuss the ontological ventures of the last decades. We limit ourselves to noting that we consider these ventures very problematic; we point only to the latest development of a well-known initiator of this movement, such as Sartre, to illustrate at least the problematic and its direction.

This problematic reveals itself in its relationship with Marxism. We are well aware that this latter has rarely been considered during the history of philosophy as an ontology. However, this paper sets as an objective to show that the decisive philosophical intervention of Marx was to overcome the logical–philosophical idealism of Hegel and to point theoretically and practically towards the conception of a materialistic and historical ontology. Hegel's role consists in preparing in his own way an ontology conceived as history, which—opposed to religious ontologies—evolves from "below" ["*von unten*"], starting with the simplest [phenomenon] and displaying the history of necessary upwards evolution to the most complicated objectivation of human culture. It is obvious that he will lay the emphasis on social being and its product, as is characteristic for Hegel; thus man appears as his own maker.

The Marxian ontology eliminates from the Hegelian all logical-deductive and teleological elements of historicoevolutionary nature. With this materialistic "correction," the synthesis of the primitive [beginning] must also disappear as the moving cause of the process. In Marx, the point of departure is neither the atom, as in the materialism of antiquity, nor, as in Hegel, abstract being as such. Such an ontological point of departure does not exist in Marx. For Marx, the existent entities must be objective [i.e., objects] and at the same time active and passive components of a concrete totality. This has two fundamental consequences. First, the totality of being is the product of a historical process; second, categories do not predicate something about a being or that which is becoming; nor are they the (ideal) principles that shape matter. They are rather the moving and moved forms of matter itself: "forms of being, determination of existences." The fact that Marx's radical position was often interpreted in the spirit of the old materialism, from which it differs

fundamentally, led to the misconception that Marx underestimated the importance of consciousness, compared to that of the material being. We shall show
later that this opinion is false. Here we only limit ourselves to stating that Marx
conceived consciousness as a late product of the ontological evolution of matter. Of course, if we interpret Marx's conception of consciousness in the ontological framework of a God as creator, or in the spirit of Platonic idealism,
we may, without any doubt, have such an impression. On the other hand,
according to materialism's philosophy of evolution, a late product must not
have a lesser ontological importance. The fact that consciousness reflects reality and on this ground renders the modifying role of matter possible is not to be
taken as a weakness, as it is by those who interpret the doctrine too literally.
On the contrary, this characteristic demonstrates its real power.

II

Here, we can turn our attention exclusively to the ontology of social being. However, it is impossible to grasp the peculiarity of this being if we do not
take into account the fact that social being originates in organic being, and
that this latter owes it existence and further development to the inorganic element. Science is beginning to unveil the preparatory stages of the passage from
one mode of being to another. The categories that are the most important
from the point of view of principles, namely, the categories of the more complicated forms of being as opposed to the lower forms of being, have already
been discovered by science: the reproduction of life, as opposed to mere
change or becoming something else; conscious adaptation to the environment
by transforming it, as opposed to the merely passive adaptation. It has also
become clear that the simpler form of being is separated from the real
emergence of more complicated forms by a leap [*Sprung*], regardless of the
number of intermediate categories; this being is something qualitatively new,
whose genesis can never be simply "deduced" from simpler forms.

Each leap is followed by the creation of a new kind of being. Nevertheless, the emergence of something qualitatively new seems in many cases only a transformation of the modes of reaction of that being which made the
change into new functional categories [*Wirkungskategorien*] possible. This
new characteristic constitutes in reality the novelty of the emerging being. Let
us consider light, which has a purely physico-chemical effect on plants (pro-
voking even at this level specific manifestations of life), while in the sight of
higher animals light develops specific biological reactions to the environment.

Thus the process of reproduction takes, in organic nature, forms corresponding to its specific essence [*Wesen*] and becomes progressively a being
sui generis; nevertheless, the traces of the ontological sources can never be

denied. Although we are unable to even outline these problems [*Pro-blemkomplex*], we wish to note that the higher development of the process of organic reproduction which, in the proper sense, is always an expressly biological becoming, also constitutes, with the help of sense perception, a sort of consciousness; consciousness is at this level an important epiphenomenon and serves as a higher organ of successful functioning.

The process of organic reproduction must reach a certain degree of development so that labor, as the dynamic and constructive foundation of a new sort of being, may arise. Here again we must omit numerous manifestations of labor that remain purely beginnings and at the same time impasses regardless of the fact that not only did a sort of labor emerge from them, but what follows from labor, a necessary evolution, namely, the division of labor. These latter stages of labor, since they are limited by the biological differentiation of the species, contain no principle of a development towards a new form of being; they remain a stagnant stability; they are an impasse for evolution.

The essence of labor consists precisely in the biological struggle of living beings against the limitations of the environment. It is not the perfection of the products that constitutes the essential moment of separation, but the role of consciousness; consciousness ceases to be here a mere epiphenomenon of biological reproduction: the product, says Marx, is a result which existed already ideally at the beginning of the process in the imagination of the laborer.

Perhaps it appears strange that we attribute to consciousness such a decisive role exactly here, where we delimit the material being of organic nature from social being. But one should not forget that the problems we face here (the most difficult of them being freedom and necessity) receive a real meaning, that is, an ontological meaning, only when consciousness plays an active role. Where consciousness has not become an effective ontological power the opposition [of freedom and necessity] cannot take place at all. Indeed, wherever consciousness has effecitvely [*objektiv*] played such a role, the result must comprise elements of these opposites.

We may rightly call the working man, the animal that has become man through labor, a responding being. There is no doubt that all work emerges as a solution in response to necessity. Nevertheless, it would be a mistake to suppose a direct relationship here. On the contrary, we become responding beings by fact that, parallel to social development and in an ever-increasing manner, we formulate in questions our necessities, and determine the means available to satisfy them. It is in answer to these necessities that we ground and enlarge our activity through the manifold of mediations. Thus, not only the answer but also the question is the product of the consciousness that governs this activity. Nevertheless, the answering does not cease to be ontologically primary in this moving complex. Material necessity, as the moving force of the individual and social reproduction processes, really sets in motion first labor with its complexity, and all mediations are ontological only to the extent to which they satisfy this material necessity.

(. . . *The chain reaction resulting from our "responding" transforms our relationship with nature and society and allows the unfolding of our capacities by liberating and subduing the forces of nature.*)

The possibility of the development of labor and of the working man is given ontologically with labor itself. If we add to this ontological characteristics of labor the consequences of the active and conscious transformation of the milieu — as opposed to a passive adaptation to it — labor becomes not only the means that allows the expression of the particularities of social being, but it will be, ontologically speaking, the model for this new kind of entity.

The more we observe the functioning of labor, the clearer this characteristic (viz., labor as model and transforming agent of the milieu) becomes. Labor consists of teleological positionings that activate causal series. This simple statement of fact eliminates a millenial ontological prejudice. Contrary to causality viewed as equivalent to laws which spontaneously govern the transformation of all beings into their general expression, teleology is always a mode of positioning originating in a consciousness. This teleology can activate only causal series moving in definite directions. Since earlier philosophies did not recognize teleological positionings as a specific characteristic of social being, they had to invent on the one hand a transcendental subject, and on the other hand a special efficiency responsible for teleological connections that would correspond to those developments that have, in nature and in society, a teleological character. What is decisive here is the double aspect of teleology: although in a society [*Gesellschaft*] that has become a real collectivity [*gesellschaftlich*], the majority of those activities whose totality make the whole [of the society] function are teleological in origin, their real existence — whether these activities are isolated or form an ensemble — consists in causal connections, which can under no circumstances be teleological.

If we consider labor as a model for social praxis, any such praxis unites in itself this opposition. On the one hand, this praxis consists in conflicting decisions [*Alternativentscheidung*], because, when acting, every individual has the choice of acting or abstaining from action. Every social act, therefore, arises from choices directed towards future teleological positionings. Social necessity can realize itself only in an often anonymous pressure on individuals, who are then compelled to carry out their decisions following a specific direction. Marx describes this situation correctly in the following way: men are forced by circumstances, "under the threat of perishing," to act in a certain way. However, men have to carry out their acts, in the final analysis, themselves, even if, in doing so, they go against their convictions.

All the real problem complexes of men living in a society can be deduced from those inevitable situations (the more complicated problems from more complicated situations) that we used to call freedom. Without transgressing the realm of labor taken in its proper sense, we may refer to the categories of value and obligation [Sollen]. Nature does not know either. The transformation of being from one state to another that takes place in organic nature obviously has nothing to do with values. In organic nature, where the process of reproduction means, ontologically speaking, adaptation to the environment, even if we may speak of it as successful or unsuccessful [adapation], nonetheless this alternative, from the ontological point of view, never goes beyond the limits of mere transformation [Anderssein]. With regard to labor, the situation changes. Generally speaking, in our way of knowing, we make a clear distinction between the existence of objects in themselves and their being-for-us [Fürunssein], which is merely thought in the process of knowing. But in labor, the being-for-us of the product of labor realizes in itself its objective ontological characteristic and becomes exactly that being through which, when properly thematized, the product can fulfill its social functions. It is in this way that the product becomes valuable (in case of failure, valueless). Values may arise only when the being-for-us becomes effectively an object. The fact that on a higher level of social development [Gesellschaftlichkeit] these objects may take ideal forms [geistigere Formen] does not eliminate the fundamental significance of this ontological genesis.

The same is true for obligation. Obligation implies those human attitudes that are determined through social ends (and not only through mere natural or spontaneous human inclinations). Even if we transfer this dynamic structure to a purely ideal domain, we find there no decisive ontological change. (Lukács stresses here the distinction between the ontological and the epistemological approach. The epistemological method is not only unable to detect the elementary form in a higher realization or to show the way from an initial intellectual attitude to a later one, but the elementary and the higher ontological forms appear from the epistemological standpoint as contradictions.)

Looking at the totality of the process of labor from the point of view of the working subject, it becomes clear that although the subject consciously carries out the teleological positionings, nonetheless he can never be in a position to weigh all the conditions of his activity, and therefore to consider all its consequences. Naturally, this does not prevent the subject from acting. Yet, there are innumerable situations in which one has to act even at the risk of perishing, though one is conscious of being able to control only a very small portion of the circumstances.

This situation, which appears to be an impasse [*unaufhebbare*], has two important consequences. (*On the one hand the internal dialectic of the ever-increasing perfection of labor, which leads to the widening of its scope and to its greater ramification.*) On the other hand, in this process of development, labor's fundamental problem remains unchanged, insoluble; namely, the impossibility of knowing all the circumstances [necessary for a decision]. This ontological characteristic of labor, parallel with the growth of labor, awakens in us the experience of a transcendental reality, whose unknown power we then try somehow to dominate and use to our advantage. There is no room here to deal with the various forms of magic and religious beliefs that are the outgrowth of this situation. Nevertheless, we mention them, although they are only one of the sources of ideological manifestations. We mention them for another reason also: labor is not only an objective ontological model for every human activity, but it is, in the cases mentioned above, the direct model [*Vorbild*] for the divine creation and for a reality produced through the *telos* of an all-knowing creator.

Work is a conscious positioning and hence presupposes the concrete knowledge of ends and means, even if that knowledge remains incomplete. As has been shown, development and improvement belong to the essential and ontological characteristic of labor; that is, how labor perfects itself or calls into being a higher order of social structure. Perhaps the most important aspect of this differentiation is witnessed in the movement towards independent status of preparatory labor, which is always connected somehow with the knowledge of the sepration of ends from means within labor. Mathematics, geometry, physics, chemistry, etc., were originally parts, moments, of this preparatory process of labor. Slowly these parts grew into independent domains of knowledge without completely losing their initial function. The degree of universality and independence of these sciences is in direct proportion to the universality and independence of labor.

Such differentiation is already a relatively high form of the division of labor. However, it is still only the most elementary consequence of the development of labor. Yet even before the division of labor had reached its full development, this phenomenon had already appeared in some form during the period when men collected only the necessary goods [*Sammelperiod*], as in hunting.

The most important thing that we should notice here is the emergence of a new form of teleological positioning [*teleologische Setzung*]. The task is no longer to cultivate a piece of land [*ein Stück Natur*] according to plans set down by men, but to motivate one man (or many) to carry out teleological positioning [plans] in a way laid down beforehand. Although a work may be very different from what is characteristic for the division of labor, already this can have only one main purpose and the means have to be found to insure the unity of the plan [*Zielsetzung*] in the preparation and execution of labor. Therefore, these new teleological positionings [purposive acts] must be efficacious simultaneously with the division of labor and remain an indispensable means in any division of labor. With higher social differentiation and the emergence of classes having contrary interests, these sorts of teleological positionings become the ideal [*geistig-struktive*] ground of what Marxism calls ideology. For ideology supplies the framework for the conflicts that result from the antagonism between more developed systems of production; these ideological structures then enable us both to be conscious of these conflicts and to struggle against them.

Social life is permeated with such conflicts. They extend from those arising in everyday life, which are solved in individual labor, to those serious problems that up to now humanity has endeavored to overcome in its great social upheavals. The most characteristic type of these conflicts exhibits essentially the same trends everywhere: as it was indispensable for labor to know natural processes in order to successfully develop an interchange [*Stoffwechsel*] between nature and society, in the same way a certain knowledge of human nature and personal and social relationships is necessary to make us sensitive so that we fulfill the desired teleological positionings. How morals, traditions, customs, and myths arose at the beginning from knowledge that originated in the necessities of life, and later, how they became rational ways of knowing, i.e., sciences, in *Fontana's* words, is a complicated question [*ein weites Feld*]. We can only point out that the sciences that emerged to influence man's interchange with nature are easier to separate from the teleological positionings that are meant to be their foundation than are those directed towards influencing individuals and groups. In the latter, the connection between the end and the epistemological foundation is much more intimate. But this assessment should lead us in no way to exaggerate the epistemological distinction between uniformity and absolute difference. There exist generalities and differences that are present simultaneously. They find their solution only in a concrete sociohistorical dialectic.

Here, we can refer only to the socio-ontological ground. Each social event originates in individual teleological positionings, but itself has a purely causal character. Naturally, the teleological genesis has important consequences for all social processes. On the one hand, objects emerge with all their consequences, which nature alone could never have produced. Think, for example, of the wheel, in which this state of affairs is illustrated on a primitive level. On the other hand, every society develops in such a way that necessity ceases to have spontaneous mechanical effects; its typical phenomenon always becomes a stronger way of inciting, pressing, forcing people either to make specific teleological decisions or to avoid them.

The general process of society is a causal one, having its own system of laws but no specific directedness. Even where people or groups succeed in realizing their ends, the outcome of their efforts is often different from what was intended. (One should not forget that in antiquity the development of the forces of production destroyed the foundations of society and provoked repeated economical crises similar to those of capitalism in its specific stages, etc.) The internal discrepancy between teleological positionings and their causal consequences increases with the growth of societies and with the intensification of sociohuman [*gesellschaftlich-menschlichen*] participation. Naturally, this state of affairs must equally be understood in terms of its concrete contradictions. Some great economic event (let us recall, for example, the crisis of 1929) could emerge as a seemingly irresistible natural catastrophe. But history demonstrates that, even in the greatest upheavals (e.g., great revolutions), that which Lenin used to call the subjective factor had greater importance. The difference between purposiveness and its results manifests itself as the real superiority of the material elements and their tendencies in the process of reproduction of society. However, it does not mean that this superiority of the material elements could in every instance produce its effects without resistance or constraint. The subjective factor arising from human responses to such influences [*Bewegungstendenzen*] asserts itself sometimes as the modifying, sometimes as the decisive, factor.

III

We tried to show in what way the decisive categories and their interconnections in social being [*Sein*] are already given in labor. It is not possible to show, even sketchily, in one conference, the elevation, degree by degree, from labor to the totality of society. (We have to omit, for example, such important transitions as the transition from utility to exchange value, and from that to money.)

[. . .]

First of all, we have to see in what consists that economic necessity that both friends and enemies of Marx failed to understand and therefore used to praise or condemn in his work. From the start, one has to stress something that goes without saying, that here there is no question of necessity, although Marx himself used such terms in his polemics against idealism. We have already emphasized the fundamental ontological ground: causality set into motion through teleological decisions where choice enters into play [*teleologische Alternativentscheidungen*]. As a result, our positive knowledge must, in this respect, have an essentially postfestum characteristic. Naturally, there are general tendencies that become visible; concretely, however, they appear in such an irregular fashion that most of the time we cannot obtain prior knowledge of their real characteristics: in the majority of cases only the most sophisticated and complex social product comes to be realized in such a way that we are able to see what direction is taken during a transitory period. Therefore such tendencies can be understood only afterwards; social insights, efforts, foresights, etc., that are not at all without importance for the unfolding of these tendencies also receive approval or refutation only afterwards. Up to now, we can notice three such directions in the evoluton of economics, which evidently were realized in spite of the fact that often they are very irregular and independent of that will and knowledge which serve as bases for teleological positionings.

First, the duration of labor socially necessary for reproduction is steadily decreasing. Today, this general tendency would be recognized by all as a fact.

Second, the process of reproduction has become more and more socialized. Marx, when speaking of a constant "shrinking" of "the limits of nature," means on the one hand that human (and for this reason social) life will forever remain grounded on the processes of nature, and on the other hand, that the quantitative and qualitative portion of purely natural elements constantly diminish both in the production and in the product; furthermore, all decisive moments of human reproduction—let us think of such natural functions as nutrition and sexuality—take in more and more social aspects and will be constantly transformed by them in their essence.

[*Third, Lukács mentions social connections, which become increasingly complicated.*]

In all these cases, we encounter decisive and important tendencies of both the exterior and interior transformation of social being [*Sein*]. Through these transformations social being acquires a specific structure: man is transformed from natural being [*Naturwesen*] into human person, from a relatively highly developed animal species into the human species, to humanity. All this is the product of a series of complex causalities arising in society. The process itself has no purposiveness [*Ziel*]. Therefore, its higher development implies the unfolding of even greater and more fundamental contradictions. Although the progress comprises the totality of human activity, it is never brought to its complete realization in the sense of a teleology: therefore, these primitive and beautiful, but economically limited, realizations, will again be constantly disturbed; this is the reason why objective economic progress always appears in the form of new social conflicts. In this way, seemingly insoluble antinomies of class struggle *[Klassengegensätze]* emerge in primitive communities; this explains why the most vicious forms of inhuman actions are also the result of such progress. Thus, in early times, slavery represents progress over cannibalism; in the same way today, the generalization of the alienation of mankind is a symptom of another change, namely of economic development, which is intended to revolutionize our relationship to labor.

Individuality *[Einzelheit]* is already a natural category *[Naturkategorie]* of being, and the same goes for species. These two poles of organic being can elevate themselves in social being only simultaneously to human personality and to human species, and, in the process of becoming progressively social, of society. Materialism before Marx could not even raise this issue. For Feuerbach, according to Marx's criticism, only the isolated human individual exists, and at the other pole there is the mute species that unites in nature *[naturhaft]* many individuals. On the other hand, the task of a materialistic ontology that has become historical is to unveil the genesis, the growth, and the contradictions as they manifest themselves in the development of a totality *[innerhalb der einheitlichen Entwicklung]*. Then it must be shown that man as producer and at the same time as product of society achieves something greater in humanity *[Menschsein]* than being a mere sample of an abstract species. On this ontological level *[Seinsniveau]* — reached by a more developed social being — the species is no longer a mere universal *[Verallgemeinung]*, whose instances remain blindly subjected to it; on the contrary, these raise themselves to the point where they have an ever more meaningful and articulate voice; they become a really existent social synthesis *[seiend-gesellschaftlich]* of individuals conscious of belonging to the human species.

IV

Marx as theoretician of this being and becoming draws all the consequences from historical development. He states that though men made themselves men through labor, history up to our time is, only the prehistory *[Vorgeschichte]* of humanity. Real history can start with Communism, which is the highest stage of socialism. Communism, for Marx, is not the forerunner *[Vorwegnahme]* of utopian speculations with regard to the realization of a projected state of affairs; on the contrary, with it begins the unfolding of those truly human forces which, up to our times, development brought to the fore and reproduced as important realizations in becoming a man; these human forces reached even greater accomplishments in a process full of contradictions. All this has been achieved by men themselves, as the result of their own activity.

"Men shape their history themselves," says Marx, "but not under circumstances they have chosen themselves." This is the same as was expressed earlier by this formula: the human being is a responding being. This definition makes explicit the inseparable unity of freedom and necessity implicit in social being with all its contradictions; this phenomenon has already been observed in labor or the inseparable and contradictory unity of the teleological decisions (with the choice implicit in them [*Alternativentscheidungen*]), along with causality and constraint, which manifest themselves in the positionings and their consequences. This is a kind of unity that is constantly repeated in all the social personal fields of human activity and takes a more and more developed and direct form.

This is why Marx can speak of the early period of the history of mankind as the realm of freedom which, however, "can blossom only in the realm of necessity as its foundation." (This realm of necessity encompasses the socioeconomic reproduction of mankind and the objective tendencies of development, as we pointed out earlier.)

The dependence of the realm of freedom on its social–material basis, namely, on the economic realm of necessity, shows how much the freedom of the human species is the result of its own activity. Freedom, and also its possibility, is neither something readily given by nature nor a gift "from above"; it is equally wrong to call it a constitutive part of the essence of man, or something having a mysterious origin. Freedom is rather the product of human activity. Although in reality this activity produces results other than those intended, effectively it broadens for freedom the realm of possibility. Thus, on the one hand, freedom increases the number of choices in the process of economic development, on the other hand, it extends man's capacities by increasing the tasks produced through man's activity. Naturally, all this belongs yet to the "realm of necessity."

The development of the process of labor and the broadening of the fields of activity have still other indirect consequences: the emergence and unfolding of human personality. This requires the growth of capacities as its indispensable ground; nevertheless human personality is not at all the simple and direct result of this growth; on the contrary, the history of their development shows that there is an opposition between these two. This opposition varies at different levels of development; howver, it becomes sharper and sharper as it reaches the higher stages. Nowadays, it seems as if the constantly increasing differentiation and development of capacities were the direct obstacle of becoming a person [*Persönlichkeitwerden*] and the vehicle of the alienation of human beings [*menschliche Persönlichkeit*].

Man ceases to be a mute [*stumm*] member of the species, even at the level of the most primitive labor. But following that, we reach a stage similar to a mere in-itself [*Ansichsein*]: namely, the active consciousness discovers the social connections bound to the ever-present economic factors. The general consciousness of the human species has not yet surmounted the particularity of the ever-present situation for the individual and the species, regardless of the great progress of sociability [*Gesellschaftlichkeit*] and the broadening of its horizon.

However, the idea of highly developed species [*höhere Gattungsmässigkeit*] has never disappeared completely from the agenda of history. Marx defines the realm of freedom as the "unfolding of human forces that are ends in themselves [*Selbstzweck*]; then, due to their worthy content, they can be valid ends both for an individual and a society. It is evident that such more highly developed species presuppose the existence of a realm of necessity so demanding that we have never encountered its like so far. Only when labor becomes completely dominated by mankind, only when it already encompasses the possibility of being "not merely a means for survival" but the first requirement of life [*erstes Lebensbedürfnis*], only when mankind has passed beyond every constraint of self-reproduction, only then will the social path be cleared for human activity as an end in itself [*Selbstzweck*].

"To clear the way" means: to acquire the necessary material conditions; to create a milieu (with its possibilities) where the self can freely unfold its activity. Both are products of human activity. The first is the result of necessary development, the second is the outcome of the proper use, worthy of human beings, of these necessary accomplishments. Freedom itself cannot be simply a necessary product of an inevitable process [*Entwicklung*], even if all the conditions of its unfolding receive in this evolution only the possibility of their realization [*Seiendwerdens*].

Therefore, there is no question here of utopia. First, because some of the real possibilities of its realization are brought about by a necessary process. We have not stressed in vain the manifestation of freedom through choice already apparent in the primitive form of labor. We have to acquire our freedom through our own acts. We can do this only because each of our acts already includes a moment of freedom as its necessary constituent.

However, there is much more at stake. If this moment did not surface uninterruptedly during the course of the whole history of mankind and did not preserve in itself an unbroken line of continuity, it could not play the role of the subjective factor in the great upheaval. But uneven development, itself full of contradictions, always had such consequences: Due to their purely causal nature, the consequences of teleological positionings enter into the world at every progressive step as the unity of contradiction arising from progress and regress. This will be, with the ideologies, not only elevated to consciousness (often to foreconsciousness) — and, corresponding to the contradictory social interests of every age, fought out — but it will also be applied to societies or living totalities, and to individuals as persons [*Persönlichkeiten*] searching for their true path. This picture, as yet fragmentary, of a world of human activities, that has value and deserves to be considered as an end in itself, comes to the fore again and again in important individual manifestations. It is worth noticing that while most of the practical innovations considered epoch making in their time disappear without trace from the memory of mankind others, having no practical value — often seemingly condemned to perish — survive and remain indelible in the memory of mankind.

The consciousness of the best among men — who are in a position to make a step forward, unlike most of their contemporaries, towards becoming really a man — insures such a permanence to its manifestations in spite of the problematic nature of its innovations. [*Lukács stresses the indissoluble link between individual and society and their interaction in the perfecting of the human species.*]

Most of the ideologies were and still are in the service of the preservation and development of the species in itself [*an sich*]. Therefore, they always adapt themselves to what is concrete and immediate [*aktuell*]; they are armed for the purpose of fighting a variety of immediate dangers [*mit gewollt verschiedenen Arten der actuellen Ausfechtens ausgerüstet*].

Only great philosophy and great art (as well as the attitudes and behaviors of exemplary individuals) work in the direction of a species in itself [*Gattungsmässigkeit an sich*]; only their examples will be retained, without constraint, in the memory of mankind; only such data are compiled as conditions of a readiness to prepare us mentally [*innerlich*] for the kingdom of freedom. Above all, what matters here is that both society and individual men reject those tendencies that threaten this process of becoming more and more human. The young Marx had recognized such a central threat in the supremacy of the category of "having" [*Haben*]. It is no mere chance that Marx conceives the climax of man's struggle for freedom in the perspective that compels human sensibility [*Sinne*] to become theoretical. It is certainly not a mere chance that in addition to great philosophers, Shakespeare and the great tragic poets played such an important role in the shaping of Marx's intellectual development and in his conception of life. (In the same way, Lenin's appreciation of the *Appassionata* is not accidental.). These examples bring to the fore the fact that the classics among the Marxists, unlike the later epigones, who were always liable to be manipulated, have never lost sight of the special kind of realizations in the realm of freedom. Naturally, they knew equally well the fundamental role of the realm of necessity.

Today, when trying to review Marxist ontology, these two aspects [of reality] must be restated: the primacy of the material factor with respect to the essence and constitution of social being, combined with the recognition of the fact that the materialistic conception of reality has nothing in common with the nowadays-so-frequent capitulation before the objective and subjective particularities [of beings].

Index